Anne Robinson
Karen Saxby

Student's Book

••• Second edition

CAMBRIDGE UNIVERSITY PRESS
Cambridge, New York, Melbourne, Madrid, Cape Town,
Singapore, São Paulo, Delhi, Mexico City

Cambridge University Press
The Edinburgh Building, Cambridge CB2 8RU, UK

www.cambridge.org
Information on this title: www.cambridge.org/9780521748285

© Cambridge University Press 2010

This publication is in copyright. Subject to statutory exception
and to the provisions of relevant collective licensing agreements,
no reproduction of any part may take place without the written
permission of Cambridge University Press.

First published 2006
Second edition published 2010
9th printing 2012

Printed in the United Kingdom by Latimer Trend

A catalogue record for this publication is available from the British Library

ISBN 978-0-521-74828-5 Student's Book
ISBN 978-0-521-74829-2 Teacher's Book
ISBN 978-0-521-74831-5 Audio CD

Cambridge University Press has no responsibility for the persistence or
accuracy of URLs for external or third-party internet websites referred to in
this publication, and does not guarantee that any content on such websites is,
or will remain, accurate or appropriate. Information regarding prices, travel
timetables and other factual information given in this work is correct at
the time of first printing but Cambridge University Press does not guarantee
the accuracy of such information thereafter.

Acknowledgements

The authors and publishers would like to thank the ELT professionals who commented on the material at different stages of its development:

ABC Pathways School, Hong Kong; Klára Banks; Paul Bress; Alexander Case; Maria Angeles Tobias Cid; Julie Dawes; Margaret Fowler; Rorror Huang; Liz Bangs-Jones; Calliope Loulaki; Justyna Martin; Rosa Llopart Queraltó; Beatriz Muñiz Rodríguez; Diane Reeves; Roger Scott

The authors of the second edition would like thank the following reviewers who commented on the first edition to help shape the second edition and reviewers who commented on the second edition: Christine Barton, Jonathan Baum, Sevim Ciftci, Philip Cordwell, Marc Danis, Marc Dennis, Elizabeth Elston, Sean Fox, Jonathan Gibbons, Ebru Gültekin, Rosalie Kerr, Begum Kirik, Rupert Procter, Gülsah Sünter, Fiona Thompson, Reyhan Yüksel

The authors are grateful to:
Niki Donnelly, Laila Friese, Sarah Brierley, Emily Robinson and Clive Rumble of Cambridge University Press.

Anne Robinson would like to give special thanks to Adam Evans and Annie Marriott for their insights and inspiration on the first edition, and to so **many** teaching professionals who have inspired and given feedback along the way. Special thanks to Cristina and Victoria for their help, patience and enthusiasm!

Karen Saxby would like to give special thanks to everyone she has worked with in production of YLE material. She would also like to thank her sons, Tom and William, for bringing constant fun and creative inspiration to her life and work.

Editorial work by Christine Barton.

Cover design by David Lawton

Cover illustration by Simon Stephenson, NB Illustration

Book design and page make-up by eMC Design Ltd.

The authors and publishers are grateful to the following illustrators:

Advocate Art (Chris Embleton-Hall 11, 28, 48, 60, 66, 93, 98); Beehive Illustration (Theresa Tibbetts 34, 36, 52, 81, 88, 101); Graham-Cameron Illustration (Bridget Dowty 26, 39, 47, 60, 78; Brett Hudson 14, 29, 32, 38, 42, 55, 59, 61, 66, 67, 74, 75, 80, 94; Pip Sampson 7, 12, 13, 18, 22, 23, 30, 32, 38, 56, 57, 59, 62, 63, 76, 77, 88, 90, 94, 95, 96, 102, 107; Emily Skinner 9, 14, 15, 19, 31, 40, 72, 82, 83, 91, 102; Sarah Wimperis 17, 37, 49, 71, 80, 89, 109; Sue Woollatt 12, 20, 26, 27, 35, 46, 49, 74, 85, 92); Nigel Kitching 6, 10, 16, 41, 44, 45, 58, 62, 63, 64, 65, 82, 91, 100, 104, 106, 108; Sylvie Poggio Artists Agency (Laetitia Aynié 31, 33, 62; Humberto Blanco 50, 68; Johnanna A Boccardo 36, 52, 53, 72; Andy Elkerton 6, 7, 20, 28, 51, 70, 77, 87; Melanie Sharp 8, 17, 40, 41, 43, 54, 67, 69, 84, 93, 97, 99, 105, 109, 110; Jo Taylor 24, 25, 58, 78, 79, 86, 87, 100)

Sound recordings by TEFL Audio, London

1	Animals	6
2	Animals in different places	8
3	What kind of hair?	10
4	The girl in the red dress	12
5	Happy or sad?	14
6	Bigger or smaller?	16
7	What's the weather like?	18
8	The biggest and the smallest	20
9	My family	22
10	Which bag is Ben's?	24
11	Things we eat and drink	26
12	Bottles and boxes	28
13	Different homes	30
14	My home	32
15	At school	34
16	Different sports	36
17	My hobbies	38
18	My body	40
19	At the hospital	42
20	What's the matter?	44
21	Where?	46
22	Why do people go there?	48
23	The world around us	50
24	Find the differences	52
25	Which one is different?	54
26	The bats are everywhere!	56
27	My day	58

28	My week	60
29	How well do you do it?	62
30	About me	64
31	Questions! Questions!	66
32	Why is Sally crying?	68
33	On your feet and on your head	70
34	What's in Mary's kitchen?	72
35	Where were you?	74
36	What did you do then?	76
37	What a morning!	78
38	Busy days!	80
39	Lost in the forest	82
40	My birthday	84
41	Saying yes and no	86
42	My holidays	88
43	A day at the beach	90
44	Which day was it?	92
45	Treasure	94
46	A day on the island	96
47	Things we do!	98
48	Round the world	100
49	Words you need	102
50	Opposites and places	104
	Pairwork activities	106–110
	Unit wordlist	111–127
	List of irregular verbs	128

Unit 1 Animals

 Say then write the animals.

1 ....bear.... 2 ....bat.... 3 .... 4 ....
5 .... 6 .... 7 .... 8 ....
9 .... 10 .... 11 .... 12 ....

 Which parts of a crocodile can you see?

What can you see in this picture? ....

 How much do you know about crocodiles?

1 Do crocodiles live in the sea? ....

2 Why are a crocodile's eyes on the top of its head?
....

3 Crocodiles swim. Can they run too? ....

4 Do crocodiles have more teeth than we do? ....

5 What do crocodiles eat? ....

6 For how many weeks is a baby crocodile inside its egg? ....

Now read and see how many questions you answered correctly.

1. Crocodiles eat fish, birds, animals and sometimes they eat people too! They do not eat grass or plants.
2. A crocodile has a long body and mouth and a long tail. A crocodile has short legs. But be careful because they can swim and they can run too!
3. A mother crocodile sits on her eggs for about 12 weeks. The eggs crack open and the mother carries her baby crocodiles to the river.
4. You can find crocodiles in many parts of the world. Some crocodiles only live in rivers but some crocodiles can live in the sea too.
5. When crocodiles swim they can see. Their mouths are under the water but their eyes are above the water. A crocodile's eyes are on the top of its head.
6. Look inside a crocodile's mouth and you can find a lot of teeth! They can have between 60 and 80 teeth. People have about 30 teeth.

 D **Read and write the animal names.**

1	It has a tail and it likes catching mice. It sounds like 'hat'.	*cat*
2	It's always hungry and it has a little beard. It sounds like 'boat'.	....
3	It's very small and it eats cheese. It sounds like 'house'.	....
4	It's green and it jumps very well. It sounds like 'dog'.	....
5	It eats grass. It sounds like 'now'.	....
6	It sings and sometimes lives in a cage. It sounds like 'word'.	....
7	It lives in the sea. It sounds like 'park'.	....
8	It doesn't have legs. It sounds like 'cake'.	....
9	It's very big and it swims in the sea. It sounds like 'tail'.	....
10	It flies at night. It sounds like 'Pat'.	....

 E **Now play the game! It sounds like ...**

Unit 2 — Animals in different places

A Answer the questions.

Which animals

live	... in the sea?	....
	... in the jungle?	....
	... in water?	....
	... on a farm?	....
can	... swim?	....
	... fly?	....
	... run?	....
	... jump?	....
	... climb?	....
are	... pets?	....
	... big?	....
	... small?	....
	... quick?	....
	... slow?	....
have got a tail?		....

Which animals do you like? ....

Are you afraid of any animals? ....

B Which one is different and why?

1 cat – horse – dog – bird   ....
2 sheep – fish – horse – cow   ....
3 dolphin – shark – cat – whale   ....
4 elephant – giraffe – whale – spider ....
5 lizard – bat – bird – fly   ....

A .... is different because ....

29/04/2013

C What's on the farm?

- a cloud
- a field
- a truck
- a chicken
- a rabbit
- a duck
- a kitten

D A day on the farm.

On Saturday afternoons, ...Tom........... and his sister, ...Marry......, go to help Mrs Plant on her farm. They carry potatoes and give the animals their food. The children ride to the farm on their bikes because it is near their home. Mrs Plant has two new animals on the farm now! She's got a kitten called Sunny and a puppy called Sausage!

1 The children go to the farm every ......Saturday...... afternoon.
2 Mrs ...Plant......... lives on the farm.
3 The children ......carry......... Mrs Plant's potatoes for her.
4 The children ride their ......bikes......... to the farm.
5 Mrs Plant's kitten is called ......Sunny...... .

E CD1:02 Listen and colour.

F Do the animal project!

9

Unit 3 What kind of hair?

A Write the answers to the questions.

1. What colour's her hair?
2. What's this? 
3. What kind of hair has he got? 
4. What's this? 
5. Is her hair long or short? 
6. What kind of hair has she got? 

Crossword:
- Across 2: beard
- Across 4: moustache
- Across 6: straight
- Down 1: hair
- Down 1: blonde
- Down 3: curly
- Down 5: short

B Talking about hair.

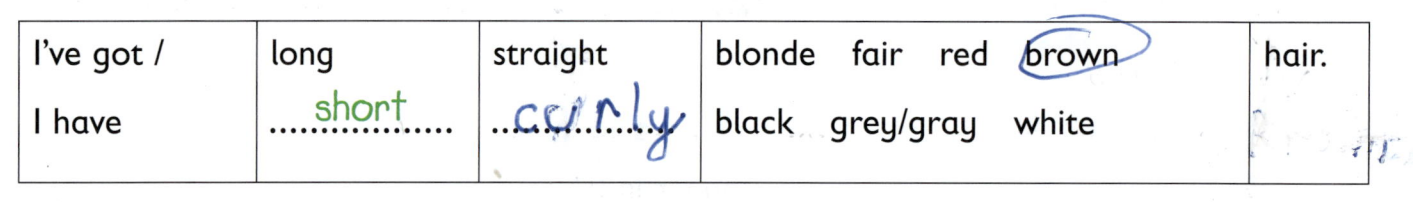

| I've got / I have | long short | straight curly | blonde fair red brown black grey/gray white | hair. |

C 🔊 CD1:03 Listen and tick (✓) the box.

1 Which girl is Kim? A ☐ B ☐ C ☐

2 Which man is Mr Scarf? A ☐ B ☐ C ☐

3 Which person is Jim's cousin? A ☐ B ☐ C ☐

4 Which boy is Paul's friend? A ☐ B ☐ C ☐

D **Alex's new film.**

Alex Top is very famous because he's a film star. He's making his seventh film now. In this film, his face needs to look very different!

In the morning, before they start making the film, Alex sits in front of a big mirror.

One person gives him a moustache and beard. Another person gives him some very long purple hair.

A third person paints his face green. Then a fourth person paints his eyes and draws lots of black lines on Alex's face.

Write 1 or 2 words to complete the sentences.

1 Alex Top is a film star and he's very ...*famous*... .
2 In his seventh film, Alex's ...*face*... looks very different!
3 Alex sits on a chair in front of a ...*big mirror*... before he starts work in the morning.
4 In the film, Alex has a ...*beard*... and a moustache.
5 Alex's ...*hair*... must be longer in this film too.
6 The colour of Alex's face is ...*green*... in this film.
7 One person puts a lot of ...*black lines*... on his face too!

E **Draw and colour Alex's face for the film.**

Unit 4 — The girl in the red dress

A Find the words for the pictures and write them on the lines.

1. scarf
2. sweater
3. coat
4. bag
5. hat
6. shoes
7. shirt
8. socks

```
s c a r f g r t w
w o s s s l s s h
e a h o h a k h l
a t i c o s i i d
t b r k e s r r r
e a t s s e t t e
r g h a t s e i s
y t r o u s e r s
```

B Find the words in the box for five more things you wear.

trousers   glasses   dress   skirt   ....

C Choose the right words from A or B. Write them on the lines.

1 In cold weather, you can wear this round your neck. a scarf
2 This is like a very long jacket which you wear when it's cold. a coat
3 You wear these on your feet inside your shoes. socks
4 People put different things inside this and carry it. a bag
5 These help some people to read a book. glasses

D Write the words from A and B in the table.

top half	bottom half	top and bottom half
scarf	socks	coat

E **Look at the picture. Write yes or no.**

1. Two children are riding their bikes in the park. .....yes.....
2. A man with a beard is reading a book. .....no.....
3. Three people are eating ice creams. .....no.....
4. The football is on the ground. .....yes.....
5. There is a small blue and white chair under the tree. .....yes.....
6. The girl in the purple skirt has got straight black hair. .....yes.....
7. Only one boy is wearing glasses. .....yes.....

 F  **Listen and draw lines. There is one example.**

 G Ask and answer questions.

Learner A: look at page 106. Learner B: look at page 108.

Unit 5 — Happy or sad?

A Write the missing adjectives.

easy thin ~~cold~~ quiet hot quick slow loud fat difficult

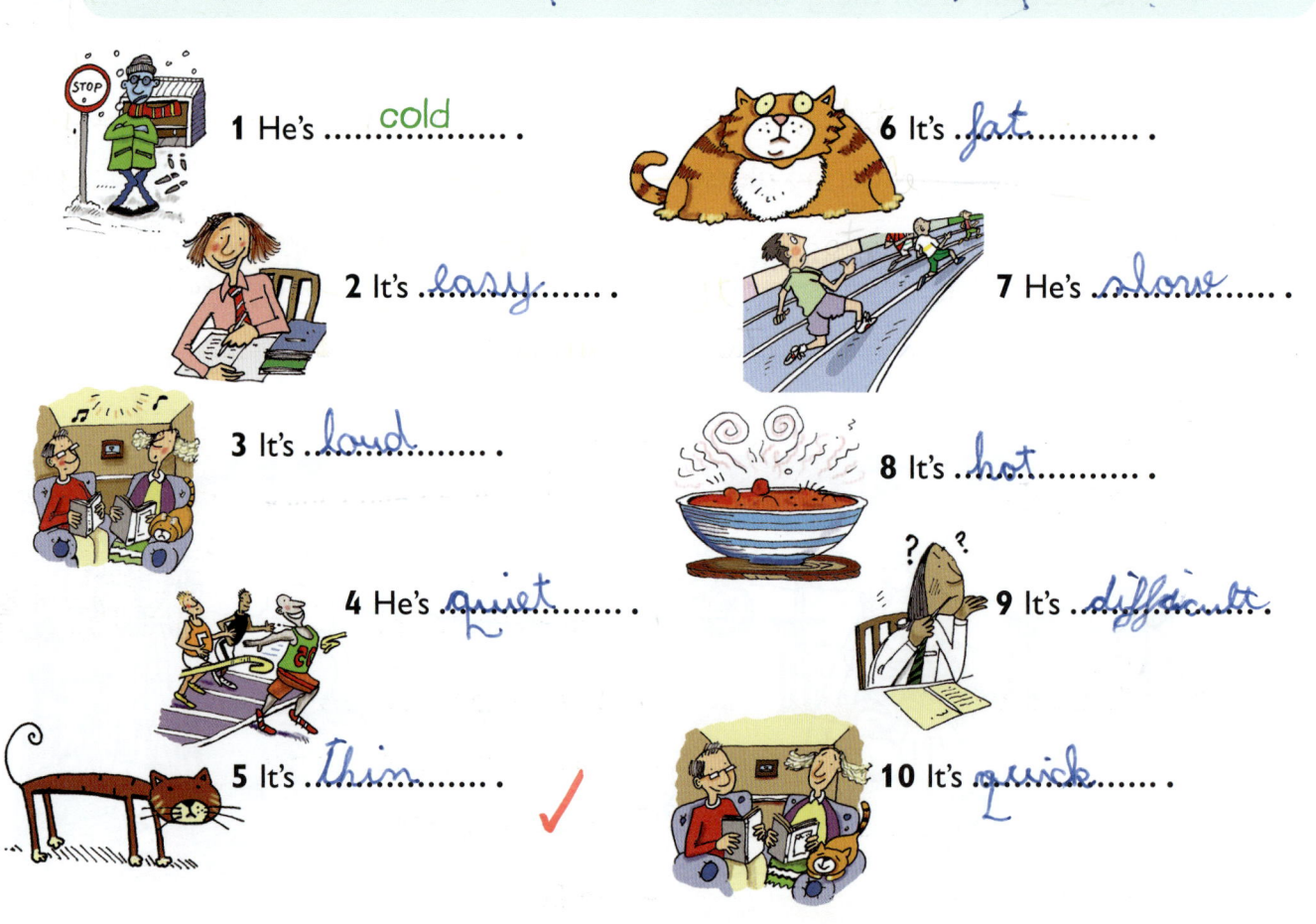

1 He's ...cold...
2 It's ...easy...
3 It's ...loud...
4 He's ...quiet...
5 It's ...thin... ✓
6 It's ...fat...
7 He's ...slow...
8 It's ...hot...
9 It's ...difficult...
10 It's ...quick...

B What does Jack say to Paul?

Hi Jack! I'm sad today. My computer is old, my new jeans are dirty and I don't like my hair. It's very long now. And I can't go outside because it's cold today. Grrrrrrr!

Hi Paul! I'm ...happy... today. I've got a ...new... computer and my jeans are ...old... but they are ...nice... and I love my hair. It's very ...beautiful...! I'm going outside now because it's ...hot... today! Great!

C Choose Vicky's answers.  Test! Reading & Writing Part 3

Paul:

Example What's the new girl's name?

1 What's she like?

2 Where does she live?

3 Tell me about her.

4 I can invite her to my party!

5 What's her phone number?

Vicky:

A She's called Sally Quick.
B No, Mary Strong is 10.
C I'm Vicky White.

A She'd like a cold drink, please.
B Are your friends funny?
C She's very nice.

A In Easy Street.
B To an exciting place.
C From her naughty brother!

A They like loud music.
B She's got very long hair.
C It's about an ugly monster.

A So do I!
B Good idea!
C Here you are!

A I can ask her.
B She's in class 13.
C Her phone's OK.

 D Listen and draw.

Unit 6 — Bigger or smaller?

 A How are they different?

Look at the pictures. Write words to complete the sentences.

1 A ......**baby**...... is younger than a ......**man**...... .
2 A ......**bear**...... is taller than a ......**rabbit**...... .
3 The ......**snake**...... is longer than the ......**ruler**...... .
4 A......**airplane**...... is quicker than a ......**motorbike**...... .

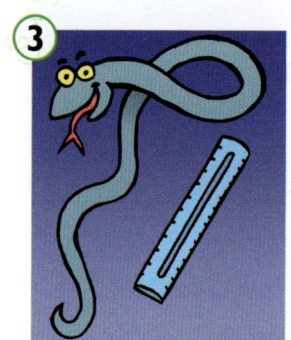

 **B Read and draw pictures of Jim and Sally.**

Jim and Sally are friends. Jim is taller than Sally, but Sally's hair is longer and her eyes are bigger. Jim has got a bigger nose and bigger ears, but his mouth is smaller than Sally's. Today, Jim is wearing jeans and a red T-shirt. His shoes are black. Sally has got a short green skirt and her favourite green and white T-shirt. She put white sports shoes on this morning.

Jim	Sally

C What different things can you see?

A

B

  D **A city and a village.**

Write the sentences in the correct box.

A city	A village
Lots of people live here. The houses and schools are often bigger. The streets are often longer. There are lots of shops here. You can find hospitals, banks and cinemas here too.	Only a few people live here. There are lots of gardens here. You can find farms, rivers and trees here too. The roads are often shorter. The houses and schools are often older.

Lots of people live here. Only a few people live here. The houses and schools are often bigger. There are lots of gardens here. The streets are often longer. You can find farms, rivers and trees here too. The roads are often shorter. There are lots of shops here. You can find hospitals, banks and cinemas here too. The houses and schools are often older.

Unit 7 What's the weather like?

A Draw pictures for the words.

a wind	**b** the sun	**c** clouds	**d** a rainbow	**e** rain	**f** snow
It's windy.	It's sunny	It's cloudy	It's wet	It's rainy	It's snowing

B Write the words on the lines.

Example This is cold and white and comes from clouds. — snow

1 This is water and comes from clouds. — rain
2 This has a lot of colours and you see it in the day. — rainbow
3 These are white or grey and they carry snow or rain. — cloud
4 You need this to go sailing and to fly a kite but it's not good for badminton. — wind
5 You can see this above you in the day but not at night. It's yellow and hot. — sun

C 🔘 CD1:05 Tony and Sally's favourite weather.

> wind   sunny   windy   raining   fly   bike   ride   kite

1 Tony likes ...sunny... weather because when it is ...raining... he can't ...ride... his ...bike... to school.

2 Sally is happy when it is ...windy... because she needs ...wind... to ...fly... her ...kite... .

D Vicky's painting class.

① Vicky is in her painting class. Vicky's friends are painting a ....*monster*...... , a ..*pirate*.......... and a ..*crocodile*..... . Vicky isn't painting. She wants to paint something but she can't choose. It's raining outside.

② Now Vicky is in the ..*library*...⁽¹⁾ . She's looking at some ..*pictures*..⁽²⁾. She came here after school. She wants to paint something but she can't choose. It's ..*sunny*..⁽³⁾ outside.

 1 Where is Vicky now?
 2 What's she looking at?
 3 What's the weather like?

③ 4 Where is Vicky now?
 5 What can she see outside?

Vicky is in the bedroom.
She can see the rainbow outside

④ 6 What are Vicky and her teacher looking at?
They are looking at their pictures

 7 Why are they happy? ....
Because they are drawing

E Which picture?

 1 Wow! Look at that rainbow!   picture ..3.. ...*Vicky*....
 2 What a great picture! Well done!   picture ..4.. ....
 3 All my friends have got an idea. What can I paint?   picture ..1.. ....
 4 I can't find a picture that I like in these books.   picture ..2.. ....

19

Unit 8 — The biggest and the smallest

 A World weather.

Complete the sentences with words from the box.

| coldest   sunniest   wettest   windiest   hottest |

1 The ......**coldest**...... place in the world is Antarctica.
2 The ......**wettest**...... place in the world is a town in India. It rains there a lot!
3 The ......**hottest**...... place in the world is Libya in Africa. It was 57°C there one day.
4 Antarctica is the ......**windiest**...... place too. The wind there is the strongest in the world!
5 It's always sunny in Arizona. It's the ......**sunniest**...... place in America.

B Our animal world.

| African elephants   snake   Hippos   Blue whales   Giraffes |

1 ......**Giraffes**...... are the tallest animals in the world. They live in Africa and they are the animals with the longest necks.
2 ......**African elephants**...... are the biggest land animals. They live in Africa too.
3 ......**Blue whales**...... are the biggest animals in the world. They live in the sea.
4 You can see the longest ......**snake**...... in the world in a zoo in Indonesia. It is about 15 metres long!
5 ......**Hippos**...... live in Africa too. They have the biggest mouths of all the animals in the world!

C Animals in cold parts of the world.

Read the text. Choose the right words and write them on the lines.

Example	Not many animals live ......**in**...... the coldest countries of the world, but animals like bears can live in very cold places.		in	after	under
1	Bears ..**sleep**.... when the weather is very cold.	1	(sleep)	sleeping	sleeps
2	They do not wake ..**up**........ and they do not eat. When it gets too cold, some birds fly to warmer	2	(up)	with	by
3	countries. It ...**is**...... easier for the birds to find	3	be	are	(is)
4	food there. There is a kind ..**of**........ rabbit that	4	(of)	from	off
5	is called a *snowshoe hare*. This animal ..**has**...... brown fur in warmer weeks, but when the weather is cold, its fur goes white.	5	(has)	having	have

 D Let's talk about you.

1 Who's the oldest / youngest person in your family?
2 Who's the tallest / cleverest person in your family?
3 Which is the biggest / nicest city in your country?
4 Which is the loudest / quietest room in your house?
5 What's the easiest / most difficult animal to draw?

the oldest: Bica
the youngest: Mama
the tallest: step father
the cleverest: Mama
the biggest: father
the nicest: mother
the loudest: Mama
the quietest: step father
the easiest: bear
the most difficult: lion

 E Our class.

1 ....**Theacher**........ is the oldest person in our class.
2 ....**Anne-Marie**.. is the youngest person.
3 ......**Max**............ is the tallest person here.
4 The person with the longest hair is ...**Raisa**........ .
5 The person with the biggest hands is ...**Gabi**........ .
6 The person with the smallest feet is ...**Catinca**........ .
7 The quickest runner is ...**My I am**........ .

 F Let's write adjective poems!

21

Unit 9 My family

A 🔊 CD1:06 **Who are they?**

Listen and draw lines.   Bill and Mary Rice

John and Anna Page   Sam and Vicky Rice

Jane (13)   Sue (11)   Ben (12)   Peter (5)

B **Read about Jane. Write the family words on the lines.**

I've got a ……… *sister* ……… . She's called Sue. My ……*mother*……'s name is Anna and my ……*father*……'s name is John. Bill and Mary are my ……*grandparents*…… I've got two ……*cousins*…… . Their names are Ben and Peter. Their parents (Sam and Vicky) are my ……*aunt*…… and my ……*uncle*…… .

C **Find the words in the box and write them on the lines.**

children   dad   grandpa   family   mum   grandma   parents   grandparents

1 father ……*dad*……
2 mother ……*mum*……   3 mother and father ……*parents*……
4 grandfather ……*grandpa*……   5 grandmother ……*grandma*……
6 grandmother and grandfather ……*grandparents*……
7 My mother, father, brother and me My ……*family*……
8 My son and daughter My ……*children*……

D Read the story. Write some words to complete the sentences about the story. You can use 1, 2 or 3 words.

Hello! My name's Ben. I live in a big town with my dad, my mum and my brother, Peter. He's younger than me. He's 5 and I'm 12. On our last holiday, Dad drove us in our car to my grandparents' house. I love going to see them because they live on a farm that's near the sea.

Example

Ben and his family ....*live*........ in a big town.

1 Peter is Ben's ....*brother*..... .
2 Ben and his family went by ....*car*........ to see Ben's grandparents.
3 Ben's grandmother and grandfather live near the sea on ...*a farm*....... .

On the first day of our holiday, Peter asked, 'Can we go and look at the horses, Grandpa?' 'Yes, but be careful!' Grandpa said. 'Two of the horses have got babies.' Grandma smiled and said, 'Don't go too near them and be very quiet.' Peter and I loved the baby horses! They had funny thin legs and beautiful big brown eyes. They always stood next to their mothers. My brother and I helped my grandfather with the horses every day on that holiday. On Saturday afternoon, we rode on the biggest horse's back. It was very exciting!

4 Ben's brother wanted to ......*look at*.................................. at the horses.
5 Two of the horses on the farm had ....*babies*.................... .
6 The baby horses had ..*big brown*........................... eyes.
7 Peter and Ben went for a ride on ...*horse back*..... on Saturday afternoon.

E Let's talk about you and your family. ✓

Unit 10 Which bag is Ben's?

A Who am I talking about?

Ben　　Daisy　　Mr Moon　　Tom　　Bill　　Jim

B 🔘 CD1:07 Listen and draw lines.

C 🔘 CD1:07 Answer Ben's questions.

1 What ......*colour*...... is your school bag?

....

2 What's your favourite .... ?

....

3 Who's your .... friend?

....

4 Have you got any .... ?

....

5 What do you like .... ?

....

D Ten questions quiz!

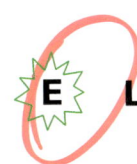

E Listen and look. Write *yes* or *no*. Test! Reading & Writing Part 2

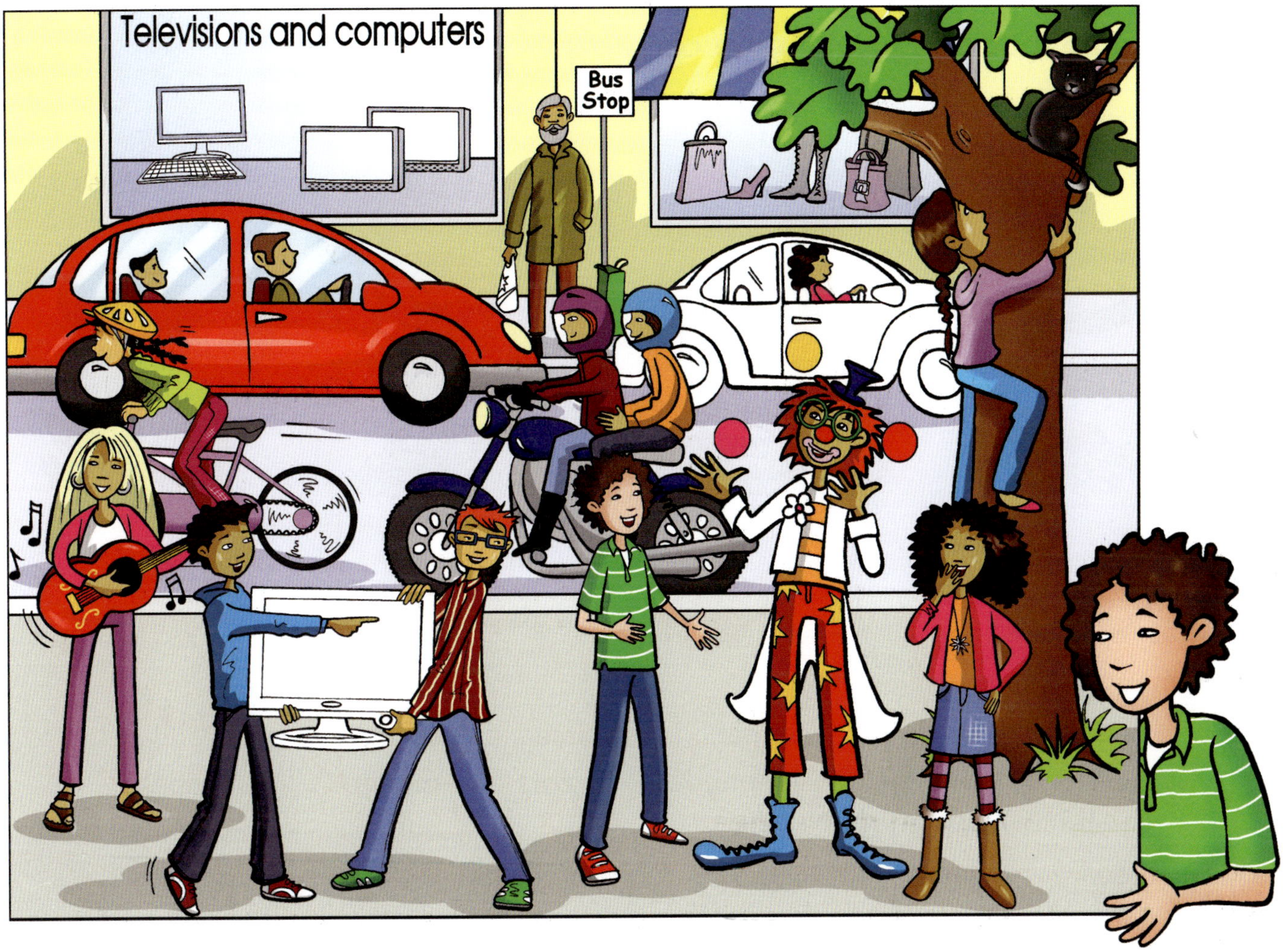

Examples:

One of the boys with the computer is pointing at the clown. ......yes......

Only one person is riding on the motorbike. ......no......

1 The clown is standing between two children. ......yes......

2 The bigger car is in front of the smaller car. ......yes......

3 A woman is waiting at the bus stop. ......no......

4 Two girls are climbing the tree. ......no......

5 There is more than one television in the shop window. ......yes......

6 A grown-up is playing a red and yellow guitar. ......yes......

F Colour that car!

G Play the game! Whose is which?

Unit 11 — Things we eat and drink

A Put the food and drink in the correct place.

coconut	lime	burger	coffee	beans	bread
pasta	chicken	lemonade	carrots	mango	grapes
apple	sausages	tea	eggs	milk	soup
pear	juice	cheese	oranges	ice cream	fish
water	pea	onions	lemon	rice	watermelon

chicken
sausages
burger

juice — tea
water — coffee
milk
lemonade

coconut — mango
apple — lime
pear — grapes
orange — watermelon
lemon — lemon

pea
onions
carrots
beans

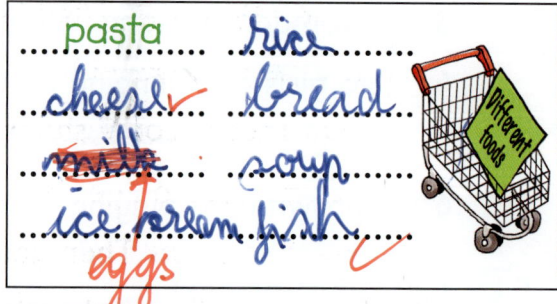
pasta — rice
cheese — bread
milk — soup
ice cream — fish
eggs

B Which one is different? Why?   hot/cold meat/fruit green/orange eat/drink

Example: Soup is different. Soup is hot. Orange juice, lemonade and ice cream aren't hot. They're cold.

C Choose the correct words and write them on the lines.

bananas   soup   a sandwich    pineapple   cheese   coffee

Example

You find this yellow fruit on trees. Monkeys like them a lot. ....bananas..........

1 Some people put milk and sugar in this hot drink. ....coffee..........

2 You can eat or drink this from a bowl or from a cup. ....soup..........

3 You make this with bread and you can put meat or salad inside. ....a sandwich..........

4 People make this from milk and it's often yellow or orange. ....cheese..........

5 This fruit is yellow inside. You can eat it and you can make juice from it too. ....pineapple..........

D Read the text. Choose the right words and write them on the lines.

Test! Reading & Writing Part 6

Fries

Example You can go to a café to ......have...... lunch in many countries of the world and eat fries there. Many people have fries at home too.

1 Some people have fries ......every...... day for lunch or dinner. They eat them with food like

2 burgers, chicken or fish. You can ......buy...... hot fries in some shops and eat them in the

3 street. You can get bags ......from...... cold fries in supermarkets. Then you can take them back

4 home and cook them ......there...... Some people make fries from potatoes. English people

5 ......call...... fries 'chips'!

	have	be	do
1	every	most	all
2	buying	buy	buys
3	from	off	of
4	here	there	where
5	calls	call	called

27

Unit 12 — Bottles and boxes

A What do we put in … ?

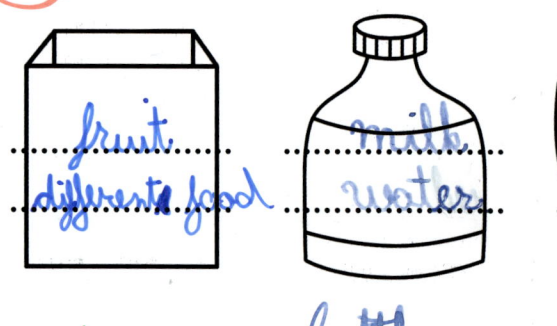

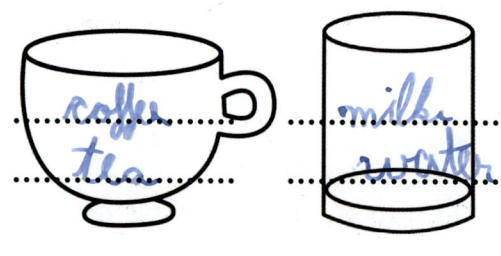

fruit, different food / milk, water / soup, cereals / coffee, tea / milk, water

a box   a  bottle   a bowl   a cup   a glass

B CD1:08 Listen and colour and draw.    Test! Listening Part 5

C Complete the sentences about the picture in B.

round   floor   table   boxes   bowl   square

1 Three people are standing near a ...**table**... in a supermarket.
2 Most of the bottles and ...*boxes*... are on the shelves.
3 The biggest box is on the ...*floor*... and it is closed. ✓
4 The ...*square*... bottle is next to the bigger bowl.
5 Four glasses are between the ...*round*... bottle and the smaller ...*bowl*... .

D The birthday party.

Dad's birthday party!
I must
1 phone: .... Jim
2 buy: .... bottles of lemonade
3 wash: the three purple ....
4 choose: some great ....
5 find: my ....

E Read and draw the birthday party table.

Draw a big table in the box.

Put these things on the table: glasses, bowls, bottles.

On the outside of one of the bottles, write what is inside.

Draw a big birthday cake.

Draw a birthday present on the floor.

Colour the picture.

Unit 13 — Different homes

A Draw lines between the words in the boxes and picture A.

door   leaves   trees   wall   roof   chimney

window   basement   balcony   stairs   mat   grass

B Find the differences between the pictures.   Test! Speaking Part 1

C Read the text and choose the best answer.

Example
Sally: Hi Tony! Do you want to come and see our new flat on Saturday?
Tony: (A) Yes please!
  B Saturday was OK.
  C No, it wasn't.

Questions
1 Tony: Where is the flat?
  Sally: A It's very big.
    B It's by the sea. ✓
    C It's going home.

2 Tony: And which floor is it on?
  Sally: A It's on the fifth floor.
    B It's got five floors.
    C There's a mat on the floor.

3 Tony: What can you see from the windows?
  Sally: A When they're open.
    B Lots of things.
    C Yellow and blue.

4 Tony: Has the flat got a lift?
  Sally: A Yes, there are.
    B Yes, he is.
    C Yes, it has. ✓

5 Tony: Can I bring Jack with me?
  Sally: A Me too!
    B Good idea!
    C Come on!

6 Sally: And we can all play computer games!
  Tony: A We're good at those!
    B She's called Daisy.
    C What's the matter?

Complete the sentences about the conversation.
You can use 1, 2 or 3 words.

1 On Saturday, Tony is going to his ....*cousin*.........'s new flat.
2 The flat is next to .....*sea*..................... .
3 You can go up to the flat in ....*a lift*.................... .
4 Tony's friend ....*Jack*................. is going with him on Saturday.
5 They can play ....*computer*................ very well.

 D Different places.

Unit 14  My home

A Jack's home.

My ....*name*.... is Jack Fine.
My ....*adress*.... is 78, Garden Road. I live in a ....*house*.... in a village called Well. Our home has six ....*rooms*.... . We've got a kitchen, a living room and a dining room downstairs and two bedrooms and a bathroom upstairs.

people
address   rooms
tree   name
house

B  Now write about your home.

I live in ...*an apartment*... (an apartment / a flat / a house)
My address is ...*35, Tucla Bucharest*...
I live in ...*a village*... (a village, a town, a city, the countryside)
Our home has ...*four*... rooms. We've got a ...*kitchen,*...
...*a livingroom, bedroom, bathroom*...
....

C CD1:09 Listen and write. There is one example.  Test! Listening Part 2

Ben's grandmother's home

Colour: blue and ....*white*....
1 Number of bedrooms: ....
2 Address: .... Bank Road
3 Name of village: ....
4 Favourite room: ....
5 House is near: ....

D Say and spell *chicken* and *kitchen*!

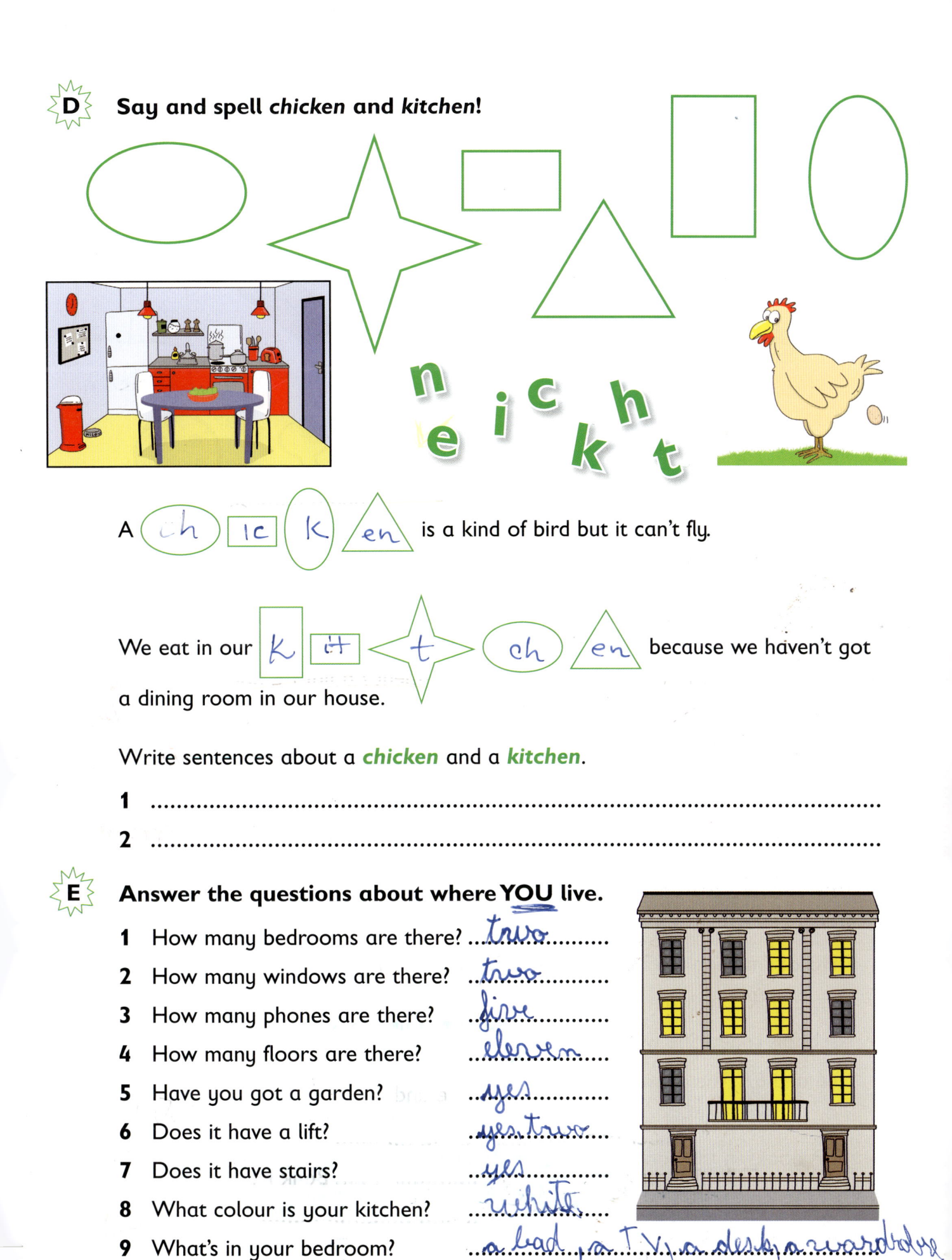

A ch ic k en is a kind of bird but it can't fly.

We eat in our k it t ch en because we haven't got a dining room in our house.

Write sentences about a *chicken* and a *kitchen*.

1 ....
2 ....

E Answer the questions about where YOU live.

1 How many bedrooms are there? ...two...
2 How many windows are there? ...two...
3 How many phones are there? ...five...
4 How many floors are there? ...eleven...
5 Have you got a garden? ...yes...
6 Does it have a lift? ...yes, two...
7 Does it have stairs? ...yes...
8 What colour is your kitchen? ...white...
9 What's in your bedroom? ...a bed, a TV, a desk, a wardrobe...
10 What's in your living room? ...a sofa, a TV, a bookcase...

F Draw and describe! My dream house.

33

Unit 15 At school

A Choose the right words and write them on the lines.

1 This is on the classroom wall and the teacher writes on it. …a board…
2 These are in books. They often have small numbers on them at the bottom. …pages…
3 When you make a mistake with your pencil, you need this. …a rubber…
4 Your teacher sometimes puts these at the end of correct answers in your homework. …ticks…
5 Look at these to find roads and rivers and towns. …maps…

B Read the story. Choose a word from A. Write the correct word next to numbers 1–6. There is one example.

Test! Reading & Writing Part 4

Hello! I'm Nick. On Tuesday, our teacher, Mrs Day, wasn't in the classroom. Our …music… teacher, Mr Skip, came in and said, 'Mrs Day is making a film about schools today. She wants you to read and answer the questions on (1) …talked… 66 and 67.' The questions were about the longest rivers in the world. I was (2) …happy… because I know a lot about rivers. Mr Skip (3) …pointed… to three big books in the bookcase. 'The (4) …maps… in those books show all the rivers in the world,' he said. 'Find the answers in them.' At the end of the lesson, Mr Skip took our books. Mrs Day came back to school on Thursday. She (5) …talked… about the film then she gave us our books back. There were lots of (6) …ticks… but no crosses at the end of my answers!

Now choose the best name for the story. Tick one box.

Nick sees a film ☐
Nick gets the right answers ☑
Mr Skip's music lesson ☐

C 🎧 CD1:10 **Listen and draw lines. There is one example.** Test! Listening Part 1

Alex   Daisy
Jack   Kim
        Tony
Paul   Fred

D Find the three sentences with mistakes.

1 The boy with the green T-shirt is reading a book.
2 Both of the boys who are drawing on the board have got white shoes.
3 Two of the boys are wearing yellow sweaters.
4 The book that's closed is under the table.
5 The picture of the train is above one boy's head.

E Complete the sentences about the picture in C.

1 The girl with the white T-shirt ...is playing on the computer...
2 The boy with the white T-shirt ...is picturing the train...
3 Two of the children are ...drawing...
4 The computer is ...on the table...
5 There is a ...book on the table...
6 There are ...three chairs in the room...

Unit 16 Different sports

 A Who did what?

watched laughed
shouted watched
played ~~played~~ jumped
jumped shouted
rained

I enjoyed Saturday! I ....played.... tennis in the morning and .... a DVD in the afternoon. In the evening, our dog .... in some water. Dad .... 'Don't do that!' But it was funny. I .... a lot!

Sunday was OK. I .... hockey in the morning and I .... a football game on TV in the afternoon. But my mouse .... out of its box in the evening and Mum .... 'Help!' It .... a lot too.

 B 🔊 CD1:11 **What did Peter do last week? Listen and draw a line from the day to the correct picture.**

 a

Monday

 d

Tuesday

 b

Wednesday

 e

Thursday

Friday

 c

Saturday

 f

Sunday

C What game did you play? Put the sentences in the right order.

1. I played a different game one day.
- What game did you play?
- Yes, it was great!
- Was it fun?
- On Friday.
- When?
- Baseball!

D Read the text. Choose the right words and write them on the lines.

Test! Reading & Writing Part 6

Football

Example	In a lot ......**of**...... countries, football is most children's favourite sport. It's a great game!	**of**	on	in
1	In ...**every**... parts of the world, this sport is called soccer. When you play football, you can kick the ball with your	1 **every**	any	some
2	feet and you can ...**hit**... the ball	2 hits	**hit**	hitting
3	with your head, but only one ...**person**...	3 **person**	people	men
4	can pick the ball up ...**or**... catch it in their hands. Children often learn to play football at school.	4 because	than	**or**
5	You can sometimes see ...**them**... with a football in playgrounds or parks.	5 **them**	they	their

E Now have fun! Do a sports project.

Unit 17 My hobbies

A Listen and draw lines.

Sally   Peter   Tony   Jim

Mary   Daisy   John

B Write the words under the pictures. The first letter is there to help you.

1 hockey    2 s............    3 c............ 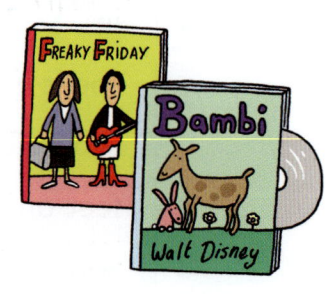   4 D............

5 a p............    6 s............ 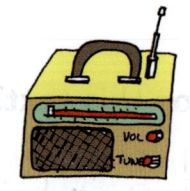   7 a r............    8 t............ t............

C **Choose the correct words from B and write them on the lines.**

1 This is like dancing but you do it on ice. ....skating..........

2 You can do this sport when you jump in water, for example
   in a lake or in a swimming pool. ....

3 There are funny stories and lots of pictures in these. ....

4 You can sit and play music on this. Part of it is black and white. ....

5 These are films you can watch at home. ....

6 Two or four people hit a small ball that bounces in this game. ....

7 You can carry this and listen to people talking or
   singing on it. ....

D **Choose words from B. Write the correct words next to the numbers 1–5. There is one example.**

My brother and sister are very different. My brother Tom is the oldest and my sister Vicky is the youngest. Vicky likes sunny weather because she loves being outside and doing sports like ....hockey.......... . When it snows, Vicky goes (1) .... on the lake in the park with her friends. Tom likes being inside and he doesn't like hot weather. He often listens to the (2) .... and, at the weekend, he watches (3) .... with his friends. The only sport Tom plays is (4) .... in our basement with his friend Bill. When he's older, Tom wants to draw pictures to go in (5) .... He's very good at drawing funny pictures.

E **What's the best name for this text? Tick one box.**

My brother and sister ☐   A day at the park ☐   My favourite sport ☐

F **Play the game! Draw your circle.**

39

Unit 18 My body

A How many?

hands .....26.....

eyes ....

legs ....

ears ....

backs ....

mouths ....

wings ....

B Write *yes* or *no*.   Test! Reading & Writing Part 2

Examples One of the monsters is flying.   .....yes.....

Three girls are watching the game.   .....no.....

1 There are more monsters than children in the picture.   ....

2 One monster has more eyes than one child.   ....

3 The tallest person in the picture is a man.   ....

4 The monsters' legs are shorter than their arms.   ....

5 A woman is looking at her watch.   ....

6 The player with the ball is standing on the ground.   ....

C My stomach and my shoulder.

my stomach    my shoulder

D Find the correct words and write them on the lines.

Example

Find this! It's between your eyes and your mouth. ......*nose*......

1 After your dinner, your food is inside this. ....
2 This is hair on a man's face. It's under his mouth. ....
3 You stand on these. They are at the end of your legs. ....
4 These are white and you have lots in your mouth. ....
5 You have two of these and you listen with them. ....
6 This is under your head and above your shoulders. ....

searsoteethlnosehfeeteneckrstomachubeardd

The mystery word is ....

E Choose the right answer.

1 The *children* / *monsters* were the best basketball players.
2 One of the monsters is holding a *cup* / *ball*.
3 The monster that is next to the door is wearing *socks* / *shoes*.
4 The robot that's outside the house is *laughing* / *crying*.
5 There's a *flower* / *puppy* in the small monster's hand.

F The monsters go home to the moon! Listen and colour.

G Play the game! Answer with your body.

Unit 19 At the hospital

A Look and read. Choose the correct words and write them on the lines. There is one example.

Test! Reading & Writing Part 1

a dentist   a nurse   a party   a playground

movies   a picnic   a temperature   a hospital

Example

This is food which you sit and eat on a beach or on the grass.   *a picnic*

1 You go to this person when you have toothache.   ....

2 People invite their friends to this on their birthday.   ....

3 You can see these at a cinema or at home on a DVD.   ....

4 Many different doctors work at this place.   ....

5 This is a place where children run and have fun outside.   ....

6 This person helps people who are not well.   ....

B Choose the best words and complete the sentences.

1 Sometimes, when you are not .... and your body is .... , you have a temperature.

    hot well cold

2 When your mum has a .... headache, it's a good idea to be very .... at home.

    bad quiet tired

3 Be .... when you're hungry! Tony ate five ice creams on Sunday then had a .... stomach-ache!

    dirty terrible careful

C **Answer the questions.**

1. What was the last birthday party you went to? What did you do?
2. What's your favourite movie? Which famous people are in the movie?
3. What food and drink do you take when you have a picnic?
4. What's the name of the nearest hospital? Is it a big hospital?
5. Is there a dentist, a nurse or a doctor in your family?

D **Look and read. Write *yes* or *no*.**

Example   The room where the people are waiting is busy.   ......*yes*......

1. The doctor who is looking at the baby has got curly hair.   ....
2. The plant that the boy is holding is very big.   ....

Now write *who*, *where* or *that* in these sentences.

3. The man .... is talking on the phone is sitting down.
4. The comic .... the girl has got in her hands is open.
5. The place .... you can buy coffee is closed.

E **Listen and colour and draw.**

F **Play the game! Find the silent letters.**

43

Unit 20 What's the matter?

A **Complete the sentences.**

1. I've got a stomach-ache and I don't want ....
2. We walked a lot yesterday and now my ....
3. I went skating yesterday and I hurt my ....

B **Read the sentences. Write the number and letter of the pictures in C.**

1. This woman hurt her arm this morning. ......4C......
2. This boy was outside in the wind yesterday. Now he's got earache. ....
3. Oh dear! That woman hurt her hand. Now she can't play basketball. ....
4. That man does not look well. He's got a temperature. ....
5. This boy needs to see a dentist. He's got very bad toothache. ....
6. This man carried a lot of big boxes from the car. Now his back hurts. ....
7. Give that girl a glass of water, please! She's got a cough. ....
8. That man always eats too quickly. Now he's got a stomach-ache. ....

C 🎧 CD1:12 **Listen and tick (✓) the box.**

1. What's the matter with Ben?

   A ☐   B ☐   C ☐

2. What was the matter with Kim today?

   A ☐   B ☐   C ☐

3. What's the matter with Dad?

   A ☐   B ☐   C ☐

4. Why did Mum go to hospital?

   A ☐   B ☐   C ☐

D Read the text and choose the best answer.

Test! Reading & Writing Part 3

Example

Sue: Hello Tom, how are you?
Tom: (A) Fine, thanks!
　　　B　Well done!
　　　C　That's good!

Questions

1　Sue: Why didn't your brother Jim come to school today?
　Tom: A　They aren't coming today.
　　　 B　Do you mean Jim?
　　　 C　He had to go to hospital.

2　Sue: What was the matter?
　Tom: A　There's nothing.
　　　 B　He hurt his foot, I think.
　　　 C　My feet are bigger than his.

3　Tom: He jumped off a very big rock!
　Sue: A　Oh dear!
　　　 B　Good evening.
　　　 C　Here you are!

4　Sue: Is he in hospital now?
　Tom: A　No, he mustn't.
　　　 B　No, he's at home.
　　　 C　No, it isn't yours.

5　Sue: Is he all right?
　Tom: A　Yes, he is.
　　　 B　Yes, he did.
　　　 C　Yes, he has.

E Write answers to the questions about Paul.

1　Why didn't your cousin Paul come to school today?
　　He had to go to hospital.

2　What's the matter with him?
　　...

3　How did he do that?
　　...

4　Is he in hospital now? ....

5　Is he in bed? ....

Unit 21 Where?

A Write the words under the pictures.

a shop	a lift	a farm	a supermarket	the sea
a river	a market	stairs	a hospital	a bank
a beach	a mountain	a playground	a lake	a classroom

1 a _a playground_    b  ....   c 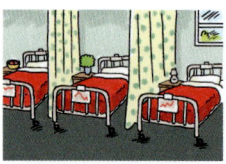 ....   d ....

2 a  ....   b  ....   c  ....   d ....

3 a  ....   b  ....   c  ....   d ....

4 a  ....   b  ....   c  ....   d ....

5 a  ....   b  ....   c  ....   d ....

B Read the story. Choose a word from the box. Write the correct word next to numbers 1–6. There is one example.

Test! Reading & Writing Part 4

Example

sunny   sandwiches   juice   give   afraid

walk   loud   lake   doctor

Fred and Jane rode their bikes to the forest last Saturday because the weather was very ......sunny...... . Then they rode to the (1) .... and jumped and played on the rocks next to the water there. They saw three ducks on a small island. 'Come here, ducks!' shouted Fred. But they didn't come because they were (2) .... of the children.

'Well,' said Jane. 'I'm thirsty. Let's sit down on the grass here. I've got some apple (3) .... in my bag to drink. Do you want some?' 'Yes, please,' Fred answered. 'And I'm hungry! Let's eat all our (4) .... too.'

When the children started eating, the ducks swam to them. 'Those ducks are very clever,' said Jane. 'Shall we (5) .... them some bread?'

'Good idea!' said Fred. 'I think these ducks are very clever!'

'I love animals!' Jane laughed. 'I want to be an animal (6) .... one day!'

What's the best name for the story?

The boy's new bike ☐

Mum makes a picnic ☐

Fred and Jane's duck friends ☐

C Listen and colour the picture.

Unit 22 Why do people go there?

A Which is the missing word?

play
books
catch
handbags
street
swim

1. You go to a library to choose ?.
2. People often go to a park to ? games.
3. You can go for a ? at the beach.
4. Markets are often outside in the ?.
5. Go to the bus station to ? your bus!

B Look and read. Choose the correct words and write them on the lines. There is one example.

Test! Reading & Writing Part 1

a supermarket    coffee    soup    a café

a zoo    milk 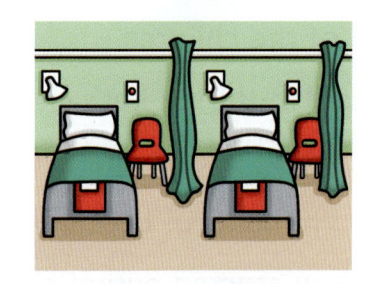   a hospital    grapes

Example

People go here to see different animals like bears and tigers. .....a zoo.....

Questions

1 There are lots of beds in this place. Doctors work here. ....
2 You can make this from vegetables then put it in a bowl. ....
3 People sit and have a drink and talk to their friends here. ....
4 This fruit can be red or green. You can eat it or drink the juice. ....
5 You can buy lots of different food in this large store. ....
6 Mothers often give this white drink to babies. ....

C Read Jane's postcard and write the correct words.

bought walked ~~town~~ tennis lunch badminton sleeping shopping father

Hi Grandpa!

It's great here!

We didn't go to the beach this morning. We drove to the town to go for a walk there. We had lunch there too. We found a café near the market with lots of chairs outside. Mum had pea soup and Dad and I had salad. Then we went to the market to buy some fruit. Mum bought a new handbag there too.

It's the end of the afternoon now and we're in the park. Mum's sleeping under a big tree! Oh! Dad wants to play badminton now! I've got to go! See you!

Love Jane XX

1 Jane and her family went to the ......town...... this morning.

2 They had .... in a café that was near the market.

3 Jane's .... had some salad in the café.

4 They .... some fruit and a handbag in the market.

5 Jane's mother is .... in the park now.

6 Jane's father wants to have a game of .... !

D CD1:13 **Listen and tick (✔) the box.**

1 Where does May's brother work?

A ☐   B ☐   C ✔

2 Where is Kim's dad going?

A ☐   B ☐   C ☐

3 Where did the children have lunch?

A ☐   B ☐   C ☐

4 Where's Bill?

A ☐   B ☐   C ☐

E Play the game! Connecting words.

49

Unit 23 The world around us

A Write *yes* or *no* next to the things you can see or can't see in the picture below.

a farm ...*no*...   fields ....   flowers ....   a forest ....
grass ....   an island ....   a jungle ....   a lake ....
a leaf ....   the moon ....   mountains ....   plants ....
a river ....   rocks ....   the sea ....   stars ....
the sun ....   a village ....   a waterfall ....   a tree ....

B 🎧 CD1:14 **Listen and colour and draw.**

C Choose the correct words from the box in **A** and write them on the lines.

1 You find these in the countryside and they often have ......*fields*......
animals in them.

2 People like climbing these when they are on holiday. ....

3 You can see water and sail here, but it is not a river or the sea. ....

4 These are parts of a plant. They are beautiful and can ....
be lots of different colours.

5 Go outside at night. Look up and see these next to the moon. ....

D Read the text, choose the right words and write them on the lines.

Test! Reading & Writing Part 6

Jungles

Jungles are hot, wet places. They are very green because it often ......*rains*...... there.

Example | rain | raining | rains

A lot of flowers, plants and animals live in jungles. There .... big rivers in a

1 | **1** was | is | are

lot of jungles. Some of .... have crocodiles in!

2 | **2** it | them | me

.... people who live in a jungle have their homes next to a river or a waterfall because they need water. The people

3 | **3** Many | Any | Every

can drink the water or .... fishing on it. People often go up or down the river

4 | **4** go | goes | going

.... boat. Rivers are like roads in a jungle.

5 | **5** in | by | on

E Do the quiz! The world around us.

51

Unit 24 — Find the differences

A Yes or no?

a

B Read the text and choose the best answer.

Example

Pat: Hello Nick! Are you enjoying your weekend?

Nick: **A** Yes, thank you.
B Yes, I've got one.
C Yes, he does.

1 Pat: What's the weather like?
Nick: A I liked it a lot.
B It's very hot today.
C No, I'm awake.

2 Pat: Who are you with?
Nick: A My son and daughter.
B The café.
C A picnic.

3 Pat: What did you do yesterday?
Nick: A We're going for a drive.
B We went fishing.
C We didn't stop there.

4 Pat: Where are you now?
Nick: A I crossed it.
B After lunch.
C Next to a river.

5 Pat: That's nice! Well, sorry, Nick. I have to go now!
Nick: A OK, goodbye!
B Well done!
C Excuse me!

C **Picture a or b? Read the sentences and write a or b.**

1 There are no leaves on the trees. ...b...
2 There's only one cloud. ....
3 The helicopter is on the ground. ....
4 The man's hair is straight. ....
5 There's a red car. ....
6 The duck is big. ....
7 The man is pointing at the helicopter. ....
8 The mat is square. ....
9 The man is wearing a blue shirt. ....

D **Complete the sentences.**

1 In picture a, there's one cloud, but in picture b, there are ......two...... clouds.
2 In picture b, the man's hair is straight, but in picture a, his hair's ....
3 In picture b, the mat is square, but in picture a it's ....
4 In picture a, the duck is big, but in picture b, it's ....
5 In picture a, the helicopter is flying, but in picture b, it's on the ....
6 In picture b, the car's .... , but in picture a, it's ....
7 In picture a, the man's wearing a .... shirt, but the man in picture b is wearing a .... shirt.
8 In picture a, the trees have got .... , but in picture b, ...

E **Let's find things we have in common!**

Unit 25 Which one is different?

A Draw and write.

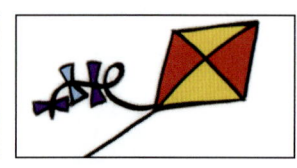

1 A ......plane......, a .... and a .... can fly.

2 The three men have got ....

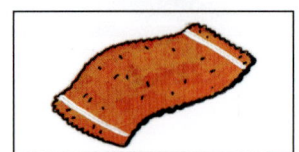

3 The .... , the .... and the .... are orange.

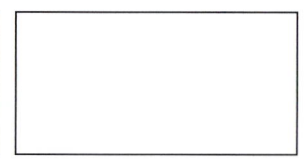

4 You can find an .... , a .... and a .... in a living room.

B Look at the pictures. Which one is different and why?

1 All of these pictures show .... but this is an ....

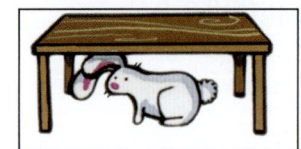

2 Three animals are .... the table but here, the bird is .... the table.

3 These people .... but this boy ....

C **Read the story. Choose a word from the box. Write the correct word next to numbers 1–6. There is one example.**

Test! Reading & Writing Part 4

Daisy ......loved...... animals. Lots of her friends had pets and Daisy wanted one too. One day she read a story in a (1) .... about a girl who had a horse. Daisy had an idea. 'Mum,' she said, 'I want to learn to (2) .... a horse. Can we have a horse?'

'Sorry, Daisy,' her mother answered. 'We haven't got a field. We can't have a horse.'

'What about a cat, then?' Daisy asked. 'My friend, Sally, has got a cat.'

'Sorry, Daisy, no,' her mother said again. 'We (3) .... in a flat. Cats like being in gardens.'

Daisy went and sat on the balcony. She wasn't happy. But then she saw a small (4) .... lizard on the ground between the two big (5) .... there. 'Hello!' she said. 'Do you want to be my new pet?' The lizard looked at Daisy and moved its (6) .... up and down. 'Wow! It's saying yes!' laughed Daisy. 'It's different from all my friends' pets, but that's OK!'

Example

loved   head   plants

grey   cloudy   ride

downstairs   comic   live

Now choose the best name for the story. Tick one box.

Daisy moves to a different flat ☐

Daisy finds a pet friend ☐

Daisy's mum writes a story ☐

55

Unit 26 — The bats are everywhere!

A Look and read. Write *yes* or *no*.

Quick   Cloud   Dream   Teeth   Sandwich

1 The biggest bat in the picture is flying below the fan.	yes
2 There's a green bat at the bottom of the stairs and it's sleeping.	....
3 Two bats are outside the house.	....
4 You can see a bat in front of the window.	....
5 The smallest bat in the picture is on top of the phone.	....
6 In this picture, there's only one spider.	....
7 The bat which is above the hall table is brown.	....
8 Most of the bats are inside the house.	....

B Listen and draw lines.

C Read the text. In each flat, write the names of the people who live there.

Mr and Mrs White live at the bottom of the stairs, below Mary Pink. The White family like cooking a lot. They often invite friends to their flat and they have dinner parties.

Anna and Bill Brown love reading quietly in their living room. They don't like living above Miss Green because she plays very loud music when she comes home after work.

Miss Green lives opposite her friend Mary Pink. They are both learning to play the guitar.

John Grey's flat is under Miss Green's. He hasn't got a car and he often emails his friends in the evening.

The newest person in this house is Lucy Blue. She lives at the top of the stairs, two floors above Mr and Mrs White's apartment.

D Play the game! Alphabet find and draw.

57

Unit 27 My day

A Ask questions about your day.

1  08:00   2  19:30   3  16:00   4 23:00

in the .... in the .... in the .... at ....

A
get up
have a shower
clean your teeth
go shopping
have dinner
go to school

B
have breakfast
go to bed
do your homework
watch TV
go for a walk
put on your clothes

When do you ...?
Where do you ...?

B Draw lines between the question and the answer.

Do you wash your dog?
Do you wash your car?  
Do you wash your face?
Do you wash your bike?

Oh yes! I often do that!
I do, sometimes!
No, never!
Yes, every day! I always do that!

C Complete the sentences.

1 In the morning, I always ....

2 In the afternoons at school, we often ....

3 In the evening, I sometimes ....

4 I never .... at night.

D Read the text about Farmer Jack. Choose the right words and write them on the lines.

Test! Reading & Writing Part 6

Is it good, bad, easy, difficult, boring or exciting to be a farmer?

Example Farmer Jack is 90 now. He worked very hard when he ......was...... young.

	was	is	were

1 I .... back and had my second
2 breakfast. I worked .... the morning, the afternoon and the evening.
3 When .... was something wrong with one of the animals, I sometimes had
4 to get up and work .... night too.
5 I worked .... day in all kinds of weather. I never had a holiday but I didn't work on Sunday afternoons!'

1 comes   came   come
2 on   by   in
3 there   it   she
4 at   after   to
5 many   every   some

E CD1:15 Listen and write. Pat's tennis lessons.

Test! Listening Part 2

Name: Pat ......Smith......
Age: ....
Day of tennis lesson: ....
Pat's class / when: in the ....
Number of children in Pat's class: ....
Teacher's name: Mr ....

59

Unit 28 My week

A 🔊 CD1:16 **Alex's exciting week.**

Listen and draw lines from the correct day to the picture. There is one example.

Monday   Tuesday   Wednesday   Thursday   Friday   Saturday   Sunday

Complete the sentences about Alex.

1 On .... , Alex climbs .... and the weather is sometimes ....

2 Alex always paints walls with his .... John on ....

3 Alex sometimes videos Lucy when she plays .... on ....

4 Alex always has helicopter lessons with his .... Mary on ....

B **It's the school holidays!**

1 Where do you go?

  A ☐   B ☐   C ☐

2 What do you wear?

  A ☐   B ☐   C ☐

3 Who do you see?   my family   my friends   my teacher

  A ☐   B ☐   C ☐

C Choose a word from the box. Write the correct word next to numbers 1–5. There is one example.

Example

| shower | sings | hide | swims |
| tennis | skating | watch | river | sailing |

Hello! My name's .... and I'm ten. My brother is called .... He's older than me.

In the school holidays, I have a ...*shower*... before breakfast every morning, but sometimes my brother doesn't! We often play (1).................. in the mornings because we're very good at sport. In the evenings, we never (2).................. movies on TV in the holidays because it's good to be outside. We like fishing in the (3).................. in the holidays too, but we never catch any big fish! We go to the beach too. Our dog, Busy, always comes with us and (4).................. in the sea! We have a boat and sometimes we go (5).................. with our father in it. I love the holidays!

D How often do you …?

sing   take a bus   do sport   watch a DVD   go shopping
listen to music   write emails   do homework   get dressed
have a party   cook   draw pictures   go for a walk

E Play the game! Who, what, when, where?

Unit 29 — How well do you do it?

A Are you good at singing? Choose the best answers.

That man sings very ....

That man is driving very ....

1 I think Peter sings very badly!

1 Why was he bad?
Do you mean Peter Green?
Did they sing it?

2 Are you good at singing?

2 It's all right.
Yes, I am.
No, they aren't.

3 Why not?
Where's that?
Whose are these?

3 My friend doesn't like driving slowly.

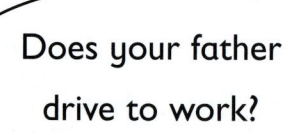

4 Yes, they rode their bikes.
Is this bus OK?
No, he likes walking.

4 Does your father drive to work?

B What do you think? Write *yes* or *no*.

1 People in my country drive slowly. ....
2 All the people in my family talk quietly. ....
3 I always carry things carefully. ....
4 My parents dance very badly. ....
5 Our teacher sings very well. ....
6 Our class is learning English very quickly. ....
7 Music is better when people play it loudly. ....

C Find words in the picnic picture.

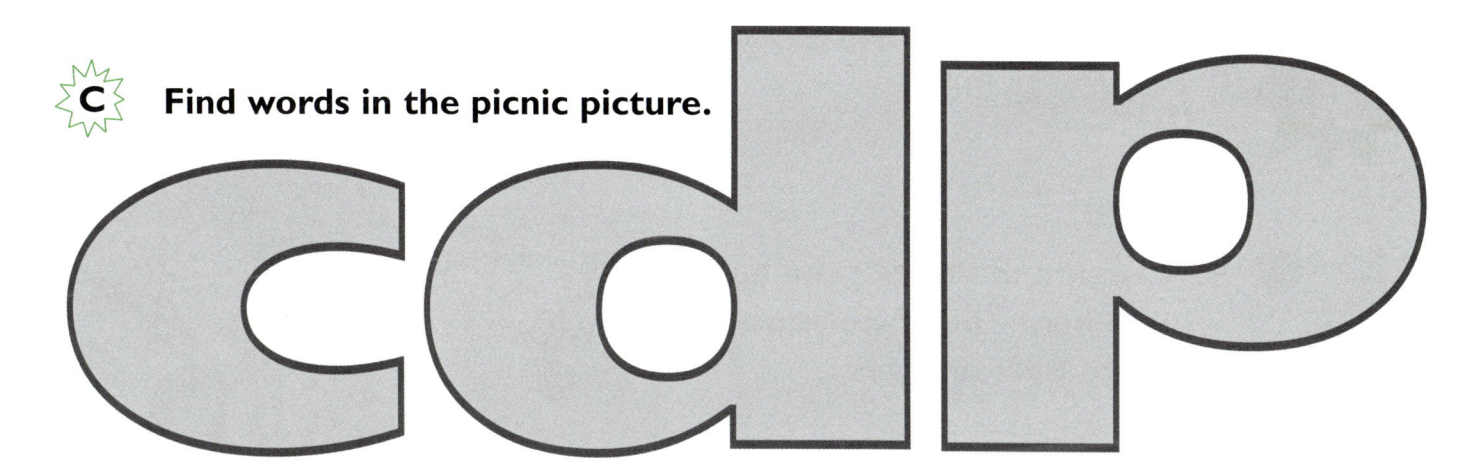

c d p

D CD1:17 **Who's doing what at the picnic? Listen and draw lines.**

Mary   John   Bill   Sally

Test! Listening Part 1

Tony   Daisy   Vicky

E **I can spell *sandwiches*!**

These have .... in them.

I like .... with cheese in them, but my favourite .... has sand in it.

F Ask and answer questions.

		Me	....
1	Can you swim?	....	....
2	Are you good at running?	....	....
3	Can you sing?	....	....
4	Are you good at shouting?	....	....

G Play the game! Draw the sentences.

63

Unit 30 About me

A 🎧 CD1:18 Listen and tick (✓) the questions you hear. Then listen again and write Bill's answers.

B 🎧 CD1:19 Answering questions.

	Bill	you
Let's talk about you.		
1 How old are you?	....	....
2 What do you like eating?	....	....
3 How many brothers and sisters have you got?	....	....
4 What kind of hair do you have?	....	....
5 What's your favourite colour?	....	....
Let's talk about your school.		<u>your friend</u>
6 Who do you sit next to in class?	....	....
7 How many lessons do you have every day?	....	....
8 How do you come to school?	....	....
9 Where do you do your homework?	....	....
10 What's your favourite school day of the week?	....	....
Let's talk about the things you like.		<u>your friend</u>
11 What's your favourite film?	....	....
Where did you see this film?	....	....
Who did you see the film with?	....	....
Do you like funny or exciting films?	....	....
12 Can you play the piano or the guitar?	....	....
13 What sports do you do?	....	....
What's the best sport?	....	....
Where do you do sport?	....	....
How often do you play?	....	....
Who do you play with?	....	....
14 Can you swim?	....	....
15 What do you like doing at the weekend?	....	....
Where do you go at the weekend?	....	....
Who do you see at the weekend?	....	....
What do you eat?	....	....

C Answer questions about the pictures.

D Read the sentences. Draw a line from the day to the correct picture.

Monday
Today was great! I rode to Uncle John's farm and helped him with the animals. We gave some food to the cows and goats. I had lots of fun there.

Tuesday

Wednesday
I was angry because it rained all day today again. I had to play 'farms' with my brother, Jim. He's only five. He's got lots of different farm animals.

Thursday
I wanted to go to the park today but I had to go to the bank and the post office with Mum. Then we went to the shop and got some brown bread. It was a very boring day.

E Write 1, 2 or 3 words to complete the sentences.

1 Bill helped ....*his uncle*........ on the farm on Monday. They .... the animals some food.

2 Bill was .... on Wednesday morning. But he played games with Jim and all Jim's .... in the afternoon.

3 Bill couldn't go to .... on Thursday. He went to the town with his mother and bought some ....

F Play the game! On my right and on my left.

Unit 31 Questions! Questions!

A Complete the sentences with words from the box.

clever   terrible   funny   ~~ugly~~   surprised   boring   naughty   angry   tired

1 This fish is very beautiful, but that fish is very ......ugly...... !
2 The food at that café is great, but the food at this café is ....
3 Why are you laughing? I didn't think that story was ....
4 Tom is very .... He knows lots of different things.
5 The teacher said, 'Stop it!' when some of the children were ....
6 I was very .... and happy when my dad bought me a new bike.
7 'Is that DVD exciting, Daisy?' 'No, it's .... !'
8 Vicky was .... when she lost her new phone.
9 'Do you want to play basketball, Peter?' 'No, sorry, I'm too ....'

B Mr and Mrs Cook's naughty daughter! Draw lines.

What did Mary do this morning? — She went to the beach.

Why is she having a hot shower?

She's a naughty daughter sometimes!

How did she get cold?

Who did she go to the beach with?

When did she come home?

Where is she now?

I know!

She's having a hot shower.

Her two new friends from school.

She came home for lunch.

Because she got very cold.

She jumped off a rock into the cold water with all her clothes on!

C Questions and answers.

What's your name, funny Earth boy?

31, Tree Street

Tom Dance

1 Where do you live?
   - On a star.
   - Her name's Vicky.

2 Who do you want to talk to?
   - You!
   - The cage!

3 Why are you here?
   - The biggest one.
   - Because I want new friends.

4 What do you want to do now?
   - To learn about your world.
   - Thank you very much!

5 Which is your star? Point to it!
   - I'm waiting for a bus.
   - It's that one! Look!

6 When did you come here?
   - Because I'm tired.
   - Last week.

D Read the text and choose the best answer.

Test! Reading & Writing Part 3

Example
Jane: Hello Paul. How are you?
Paul: A Fine, thanks.
       B I'm ten.
       C My name's Paul.

Questions

1 Jane: Do you like living in the countryside?
   Paul: A He's too quiet.
         B It's great.
         C They were surprised.

2 Jane: Where's your house?
   Paul: A It's opposite a farm.
         B It was last Thursday.
         C It's got six bedrooms.

3 Jane: Have you got any new friends?
   Paul: A Yes, there are.
         B Yes, he does.
         C Yes, I have.

4 Paul: When can you come and visit me?
   Jane: A Next to the post office.
         B Saturday afternoon.
         C The bus is better.

5 Jane: Text me your address, please!
   Paul: A Well done!
         B So do I!
         C All right!

67

Unit 32 — Why is Sally crying?

A Look and read. Write *yes* or *no*.

Ann

Tony

Sue

Ben

Mary

Fred

Examples

Two boys are eating ice creams. ......yes......

The smallest giraffe is eating leaves. ......no......

1 The man who is sitting down is happy. ....

2 One of the girls is afraid of the spider. ....

3 The robot is the one who is bouncing a ball. ....

4 Three people in the picture are laughing. ....

5 The boy who is on the ground is hot. ....

6 The spider is running up the wall. ....

B CD1:20 Listen and colour and write. Test! Listening Part 5

C Listen and draw lines.

D Look at these pictures and tell the story.

....   a ....

Sally is very ....sad.... because her favourite bear is .... She's

....

Sally's mum is .... The bear is .... now.

She puts the bear in the .... with the clothes. The .... and the

.... are wet.

Sally's mum is giving Sally the ....

Now, Sally is very .... because the bear is very ....

Write the letters under the correct picture.

a   Mum: Here's your bear. It's clean now!

b   Mum: Your bear needs a bath.

c   Mum: Look! I put your bear outside in the garden with the clothes.

d   Mum: Your bear was very dirty! Look at this water! It's black!

E Read and answer the questions.

1   What do you do when you're tired?
2   What do your friends eat when they're hungry?
3   Do you shout when you're angry?
4   What do your friends say when they see something sad?
5   Do you laugh a lot when you're happy?
6   What does your family drink when they're thirsty?
7   What do you do when you're afraid?

F Play the game! Match the cards.

Unit 33 — On your feet and on your head

A Make sentences.

You find		outside windows in some houses or flats.
	this	on your head in cold weather.
You see		on beaches.
		on your feet when you go for a walk.
		in libraries.
You put		in the sea or in a lake.
	these	at the cinema or on television.
You wear		on trees.

B Find the words in the box and write them on the lines.

Example This is green. Cows and horses eat it. ......*grass*......

1 You see this on the ground at the beach. ....
2 People wear these on their feet, but they don't walk in them! ....
3 You listen to this. It's music with words.
   a ....
4 Some people have these when they are asleep.
   ....
5 You can hold this and talk to people with it.
   a ....
6 Some men have this under their nose.
   a ....
7 You run a lot and kick a ball in this game.
   ....
8 This is hair that is under a man's mouth.   a ....

d	r	e	a	m	s	m
n	b	e	a	r	d	o
s	k	a	t	e	s	u
g	l	a	s	s	e	s
s	o	c	c	e	r	t
b	v	s	a	n	d	a
i	r	s	o	n	g	c
k	p	h	o	n	e	h
e	g	r	a	s	s	e

70

C Complete the sentences about the other words in the box.

1 You wear .... on your ....

They help you ....

2 You have to move your .... and ....

to ride this.   a ....

D Which picture is different and why? Test! Speaking Part 3

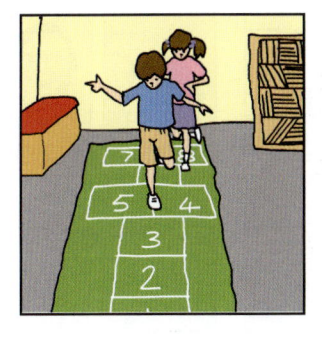

E Play the game! Plural quiz.

71

Unit 34 What's in Mary's kitchen?

A What can you see in the kitchen?

B Write sentences about the picture.

1 There are only two .... apples ....
2 There are a lot of ....
3 There's a lot of ....
4 There's not much ....
5 I can see some ....
6 I can't see any ....

C What does Mary need to buy?

potatoes   coffee   tea   rice   pasta   oranges   apples
carrots   cheese   onions   tomatoes

D Complete the sentences about the story.   Test! Speaking Part 2

72

Picture 1 Mary is at the ......*market*........ . She's buying some fruit and .... for her mum. The man is giving Mary a bag of .... John Pear is next to Mary. He's got his bike with him.

Picture 2 Mary is not at the .... now . She's walking home. But the fruit and vegetables are not in her bag now. They're on the .... John Pear's riding his .... He's behind Mary.

Write words from the box on the lines for picture 3.

| angry | market | surprised | shopping | home | empty |

Picture 3 Mary is at .... again. Her mum is .... with Mary because the bag is .... Mary is very .... 'I don't understand, Mum! I put all the .... in the bag at the .... !' she says.

Answer the questions to talk about picture 4.

1 Where are Mary and her mum now?
   ....

2 Who is outside the door?
   ....

3 What is inside the box?
   ....

4 Are Mary and her mum happy now?
   ....

E **Who says this?**   Mary   Mary's mum   John Pear

1 ......*John Pear*...... : I found these fruit and vegetables in the street. You dropped them, I think.

2 .... : Can I have two kilos of potatoes, please?

3 .... : Where are the fruit and vegetables? This bag is empty!

4 .... : Thank you! Now I don't have to go shopping again!

Unit 35 — Where were you?

A Write the places under the pictures.

a swimming pool   a hospital   a cinema   a park
a sports centre   some shops   a house

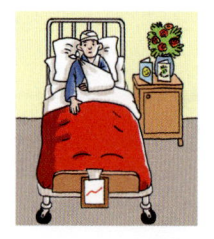

1 a hospital    2  ....   3 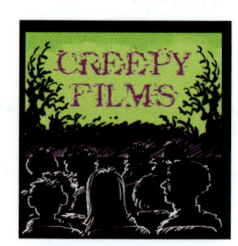 ....   4 ....

5  ....   6  ....   7 ....

B CD1:21 Listen and write where Paul was last week. Write one word on each line.

1 On Tuesday, Paul was at the ...swimming... pool with his school ....

2 On Friday afternoon, Paul went .... in the ....

3 On Saturday, Paul didn't go to the cinema. He watched .... with his .... John.

4 On Wednesday, Paul went to the .... His .... bought him some new clothes.

5 On Thursday, Paul went to the .... to see his friend's baby ....

74

C Read the text and choose the best answer.

Test! Reading & Writing Part 3

Example

Nick: Did you enjoy your holiday last week, Paul?

Paul: A It was great!
B Saturday and Sunday!
C What a nice smile!

Questions

1 **Nick:** Which was the best day?
   Paul: A Hers is the best one.
   B I can go this evening.
   C They were all good.

2 **Nick:** How did you get there?
   Paul: A There were nine people.
   B We went by plane.
   C It was very quick.

3 **Nick:** Were you afraid?
   Paul: A No, I wasn't.
   B No, I'm not.
   C No, I couldn't.

4 **Nick:** Was the weather good?
   Paul: A It was very nice.
   B I like doing that.
   C He's not in the park.

5 **Nick:** Did you take any photos?
   Paul: A I'm OK, thanks.
   B No, she doesn't.
   C Yes, forty-five!

6 **Nick:** You must show me them!
   Paul: A Good night!
   B All right!
   C Take my paints, please!

D Let's talk about last weekend.

1 Where were you on Saturday?
2 Who were you with on Saturday afternoon?
3 Where did you go on Sunday?
4 What was the weather like on Sunday?
5 Tell me more about last weekend.

boring   busy
different   exciting   great
quiet   terrible

Last weekend was
.... !

Unit 36 What did you do then?

A Past and present.

When I was young, I walked 50 kilometres in one day, Daisy. Now I only walk to the shops!

When I was a young woman, I climbed mountains, Fred. Now I only climb the stairs to my flat!

jump
called
waited
show
shout
rain
move
look
open
washed

B Look at the pictures, then complete the sentences.

1 I p.....layed............. tennis last Monday.
2 My brother p...................... all his friends last night to talk about football.
3 My younger sister c...................... six pictures with her new pencils today.
4 My big sister d...................... to some great music at a party yesterday.
5 My father w...................... a lot at the bank on Tuesday and Wednesday.
6 My cousin Jack s...................... down the river on Saturday.
7 My cousin Alex l...................... a lot at the clowns in the circus yesterday.
8 My uncle Tom c...................... lunch for all the family last Sunday.
9 My older brother d...................... six eggs on the floor last night.
10 My parents c...................... three mountains on their last holiday.

76

C On T_ _ sday or on T_ _ _ sday?

Monday   Wednesday   Friday

T ___ ___ sday   T ___ ___ ___ sday

I ………………………………….. on T ___ ___ sday.

I ………………………………….. on T ___ ___ ___ sday.

D CD1:22 What did Jim do last week? Test! Listening Part 3
Listen and draw a line from the day to the correct picture.

Monday

Wednesday

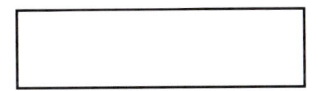

Friday

Saturday

Sunday

E Look at the pictures and find five differences.

1

2

F Play the game! Who did this?

Unit 37 What a morning!

A Choose the correct words and write them on the lines.
Test! Reading & Writing Part 1

a cup  breakfast  a bus stop  homework

clothes  a shower 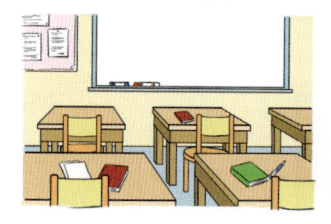 a classroom  dinner

Example

Children sit and learn in this place.   a classroom

Questions

1 Children do this work after school in their homes.   ....

2 Wait here and then a driver takes you to town.   ....

3 You eat this in the morning. It isn't lunch!   ....

4 You stand in this and wash your body.   ....

5 You hold this. Be careful! It's got hot coffee in it! ....

6 You put these on in the morning and take them off again at night. ....

B Ben's terrible school morning.

Test! Speaking Part 2

78

C Read the sentences about things we do every day. Then complete the sentences about Ben's morning.

Every day.

Ben's terrible morning.

Example I wake up.

Ben ....woke.... up late.

1 I get up and I have a shower.

Ben .... up but he .... a shower.

2 I put on my clothes and I take my school bag.

Ben .... on his clothes but he .... his school bag.

3 I say goodbye to my parents.

Ben .... goodbye.

4 I go out of the house and I catch the bus.

Ben .... out of the house but he .... the bus.

5 I sit at the back of the bus.

Ben .... on the bus.

6 I go into the classroom and my teacher is very happy with me.

Ben .... into the classroom but his teacher .... not happy.

D Complete Nick's story. Write one word on each line.

I got up and I (1) ....had.... a shower. I (2) .... on my clothes and went downstairs to the kitchen. I had breakfast with my family. Then I (3) .... my coat from the hall cupboard. I (4) .... goodbye to my parents and then I (5) .... out of the house. I walked to the bus stop and I (6) .... the bus to school. I (7) .... at the back of the bus and laughed and talked with my friends. When I (8) .... into the classroom, the teacher (9) .... very happy because I had all my books and homework. Ben came into the classroom. He (10) .... wet. The teacher shouted at him because he didn't have any books or homework!

E Play the game! The past verb game.

79

Unit 38 Busy days!

A Look at the things Sam wanted to do last Saturday. Complete the sentences.

Saturday
- play football with Paul
- do homework
- clean bike
- buy present for Sally
- email Jack and Daisy
- go to Sally's party

1 Sam *couldn't play football* with Paul.
2 He .... a present for his friend.
3 He .... Jack and Daisy.
4 His bike was dirty but he .... it.
5 He was angry because he .... to Sally's party.
6 He .... any homework, but he wasn't angry about that!

B CD1:23 Sam's Sunday. Listen and tick (✔) the boxes. *Test! Listening Part 4*

1 Where did Sam go this afternoon?
   ☐ A   ✔ B   ☐ C 

2 What did Sam do this morning?
   ☐ A   ☐ B   ☐ C 

3 Where is Sam's computer?
   ☐ A   ☐ B   ☐ C 

4 What homework does Sam have to do today?
   ☐ A   ☐ B   ☐ C 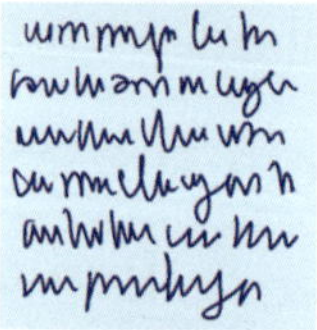

5 What number is Sally's house? 
   ☐ A    ☐ B    ☐ C

C What about you?

I like… I have to…

have/having a shower
eat/eating breakfast
go/going to school
clean/cleaning my teeth
draw/drawing pictures
play/playing computer games
get/getting dressed
watch/watching TV
do/doing homework
sleep/sleeping

D Listen, then read the story: *Mr Must's exciting letter.*

John Must was a bus driver but he didn't like getting up in the morning! Mrs Must had to say, 'Get up, John!' After breakfast every morning, he had to put on his bus driver's uniform and ride his bike to work. When he got to the bus station, he had to wash the bus. Then he had to start the bus and drive it all day. He had to say 'Good morning!' and smile at every person who rode on his bus. But Mr Must didn't want to be a bus driver. He wanted to work in the countryside. Mr and Mrs Must didn't like living in the town.

1 Mr Must went to work on his ......*bike*...... every day.

2 Mr Must said .... to all the people on the bus.

3 Mr Must didn't like being a ....

One evening, when he got home, Mrs Must said, 'A letter came for you today. Here you are!' Mr Must opened his letter and smiled. 'Wow!' he said. 'I don't have to be a bus driver now. We can go and live in the beautiful countryside.' Mrs Must was surprised. 'Can we?' she asked. 'Yes! The letter is from Mr All,' Mr Must answered. 'Listen. Mr All says, "Please come and work for me at Right Farm!"' Mrs Must laughed and said, 'Hurray!'

4 .... gave the letter to Mr Must.

5 Mr and Mrs Must can live in .... now.

6 Mr Must is happy because he can work at .... !

81

Unit 39 — Lost in the forest

A Look at the picture and read the story. Write 1, 2 or 3 words to complete the sentences about the story.

Test! Reading & Writing Part 5

On Sunday, Jim went to a lake with his mum, dad and brother, Paul. The boys and their puppy, Tiger, played on some grass next to the forest there. Paul threw a yellow ball. Tiger ran to find it in the forest, but he didn't come back again. The boys looked for him in the forest, but they couldn't find him.

Examples

Jim's family went to .... *a lake* .... on Sunday.

The boys' puppy is called .... *Tiger* ....

Questions

1 The children and their puppy played on .... that was next to the forest.

2 The puppy wanted to get the .... from the forest.

3 Jim and Paul .... Tiger, but they didn't find him.

B CD1:24 Listen and write. There is one example.

Test! Listening Part 2

	Missing animal:	.... *puppy* ....
1	When lost:	this ....
2	Boy's name:	Jim ....
3	Address:	.... City Road
4	Animal lost in:	....
5	Colour of animal:	.... and white

C Read the second part of the story. Complete the sentences.

Jim's family and the policeman looked behind the trees, but they couldn't find Tiger. 'Look!' shouted Paul. 'There's Tiger's yellow ball! Tiger! Are you here too?' There were lots of leaves next to the ball. Jim pointed to them and said, 'Look! That leaf isn't green – it's black and it's moving!' 'It's not a leaf!' laughed the policeman. 'Look! It's your puppy's tail! He's hiding from you!' Jim picked Tiger up. 'Naughty dog!' he said and laughed. Tiger jumped out of Jim's arms and ran to the ball and picked it up in his mouth. 'He wants to play again!' Jim smiled.

4 The .... , Jim, Paul and their parents all went to look for Tiger.

5 .... saw Tiger's ball on the ground.

6 Jim .... the leaves that were next to the ball.

7 The leaf that moved was .... , not green.

8 It wasn't a leaf. It was the .... !

9 Jim picked his puppy up but the dog .... his arms.

10 .... wanted to play more games!

D Read and complete the conversation about your pet.

Policeman: What's the matter?
You: I can't find my *........................... .
Policeman: When did you lose your *........................... ?
You: ....
Policeman: And what's your name?
You: ....
Policeman: Where do you live?
You: ....
Policeman: Where were you when you lost your *........................... ?
You: I was ....
Policeman: Can you tell me more about your *........................... ?
You: Yes, ...

Unit 40 — My birthday

A Look at the picture. Complete the sentences.

Lucy

1 ......All...... of the people in the picture are standing up.

2 A woman with long .... blonde hair is carrying a birthday cake.

3 There are four .... of lemonade.

4 There are two people with numbers on their ....

5 The young .... who is dancing is not wearing shoes.

6 A man with a brown .... is making a video of the party.

7 Three of the presents on the ground are ....

B Read the text and choose the best answer.

1 Alex: Hello Lucy! It was your birthday yesterday. Happy birthday!
   Lucy: A Let's go!
          B Me too!
          C Thanks!

2 Alex: Did you enjoy your party?
   Lucy: A Yes, it was great!
          B Yes, I can come today.
          C Yes, there were two.

3 Alex: Did your mum make a cake?
   Lucy: A No, my aunt made it.
          B My mother's called Daisy.
          C Put it on the table, please.

4 Alex: What did you do at the party?
Lucy: A We did it very well.
B You can make the dinner.
C We danced and played games.

5 Alex: How many people were at your party?
Lucy: A What a nice day!
B I don't know!
C They were very funny!

C Read the story. Choose a word from the box.
Write the correct word next to numbers 1–6. There is one example.

Test! Reading & Writing Part 4

Example

birthday

bought

zoo

sheep

windy

close

lunch

surprised

hid

Hello! My name's Jack.
Last weekend was my ....*birthday*.... . My parents took my sister and me to Forest Farm. Forest Farm is a kind of (1)................ where you can see and play with lots of different animals. You can watch dogs that work with animals like (2)................ and goats. I helped the grown-ups to give the chickens their breakfast. My sister took a lot of photos of all the animals. We had (3)................ in the farm café. I ate my favourite cheese and tomato sandwiches and my sister was happy because Mum (4)................ her sausages and fries. That afternoon, my dad told me to (5)................ my eyes. He took me downstairs to the café basement. 'Open your eyes,' he said. I opened them and saw all my friends. I was very (6)................ ! We had a birthday party at the farm. It was a very exciting day.

85

Unit 41 Saying yes and no

A Look at the pictures in B. Are these sentences about Picture 1, 2, 3 or 4?

1 Four people are dancing to the music.   Picture ...1...
2 The boy in the green T-shirt is smiling and pointing   Picture ....
   at a very big birthday cake.
3 A man has got a piece of birthday cake, but the boy   Picture ....
   doesn't want it.
4 The boy is sitting down on a yellow armchair.   Picture ....
5 There's only one boy and he's eating a very big   Picture ....
   piece of cake.
6 A girl is holding a glass in her hand.   Picture ....
7 We can see part of a yellow and white flower on   Picture ....
   a girl's T-shirt.

B CD1:25 Look at the pictures. Tell the story. *Test! Speaking Part 2*

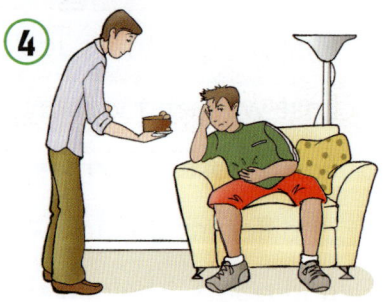

C CD1:26 Listen to the story. Complete the sentences.

1 Jack's birthday cake is brown because it has ...chocolate... inside it.
2 Jack eats .... pieces of cake because he loves it!
3 Jack's friends want to play .... with Jack.
4 Jack doesn't want to eat any more cake in the evening because his
   .... hurts.

86

D 🎧 CD1:27 Listen and complete the sentences.
Then listen again and write the boy's answers.

Fine!   Great!   Thanks.   Yes, please.   OK.

Questions   **Answers**

1 ....Would....... you ....like....... to take   ....
   some lunch with you?

2 .... are some sandwiches.   ....

3 You .... take some fruit with you.   ....

4 .... some   ....
   orange juice?

5 .... you .... to buy   ....
   an ice cream?

E Look at these pictures. What different things can you see?   Test! Speaking Part 1

F Play the game! Say thanks.

87

Unit 42 My holidays

A Let's talk about holidays.

1 Do you enjoy going on holiday?
2 What do you like eating on holiday?
3 Who do you go on holiday with?
4 What do you like doing on holiday?

a My grandparents.
b Yes, it's great.
c Playing tennis.
d Coffee ice cream.

Tell me about your last holiday.

B Read the text and choose the best answer.

1 Mr Ride: Did you enjoy your holiday, Jill?
  Jill: A Yes, please!
       B Yes, OK!
       (C) Yes, thanks!

2 Mr Ride: Where did you go?
  Jill: A With my school friends.
       B To the jungle.
       C On Monday afternoon.

3 Mr Ride: How did you get there?
  Jill: A Bring your bike!
       B I'm crossing the road.
       C We went by plane.

4 Mr Ride: What sport did you do on your holiday?
  Jill: A We went swimming.
       B You did that on Friday.
       C He has sports lessons.

5 Jill: Here are two photos!
  Mr Ride: A Oh dear! We can't.
          B Wow! They're great!
          C Excuse me, Jill!

C Jill's holiday photos. Find the differences.

Test! Speaking Part 1

88

D Read Fred's story. Write the correct word next to the numbers.

My holiday by Fred Top
My name's Fred and I (1) love going on holiday. On my last holiday I went to an island. I enjoyed my holiday a lot. We went there by plane. That was exciting too!
It was hot and (2) .... every day on the island, but at night sometimes it rained and rained.
The food there was great. We often ate (3) .... and Dad cooked fish on the beach one day too! We went swimming every morning, then we went for long walks every afternoon. I took my (4) .... with me because I wanted to take lots of photos with it. I brought some beautiful shells home. I gave the best one to my (5) .... She loved it.

sunny   love   camera
clever   pineapples   climb   grandma

E Answer the questions. Write 1 or 2 words.

My holiday and your holiday

me · you

		me	you
1	Where did you go on holiday?	....	....
2	How did you get there?	by	by ....
3	What was the weather like?	....	....
4	What did you do there?	I	I ....
5	What did you take on holiday?	....	....
6	What did you bring home?	a	a ....

F Do a holiday project! The best advert.

Unit 43 A day at the beach

A Look at these pictures. Tell the story. *Test! Speaking Part 2*

B Write some words to complete the sentences about the story. You can use 1, 2 or 3 words.

Last Tuesday, Sam and his brother Nick went to the beach. They put their towels and T-shirts on the sand and then they played football. Then, because they wanted to go for a swim, they went into the water.

1 Nick has a .... *brother* .... called Sam.
2 The boys put their things on the beach and then they ....
3 The boys went into the sea to go for ....

First, they tried to find shells at the bottom of the sea and sea animals under the rocks. Then, they saw something yellow in the water. Sam caught it and they swam to the rocks to look at it. 'It's your towel, Sam!' laughed Nick.

4 The boys looked under the rocks for ....
5 When they were in the sea, ... a yellow thing.

But Nick stopped laughing when he saw his towel and clothes were in the water too. They had to put on their wet clothes and walk to the bus. Sam had no shoes and Nick didn't have a T-shirt. The people on the bus looked at them and some people started pointing and laughing. Their parents were very angry when they saw the boys. 'You must be more careful,' they said.

6 Sam lost his .... in the water and Nick lost his T-shirt.
7 When the boys got on .... , some people thought they looked funny.
8 Their parents told them to be ....

C Look and read. Choose the correct words from the story and write them on the lines.

1 Trousers, T-shirts and skirts are examples of these. clothes
2 This is often yellow and you find it on the beach. ....
3 These are beautiful. You can pick them up on the
   beach or in the sea. ....
4 You can swim to these and sit on them.
   Some people climb them. ....
5 When you are wet after a swim, you need this. ....
6 You can go to school or to the shops on this. ....
7 These people are your mother and your father. ....

D Read the sentences. Then write words which mean the same.

1 Take something off the floor.   p _i_ _c_ _k_ something u _p_
2 Have a swim.   g _ f _ _ a swim
3 Take a bus.   c _ _ _ _ a bus
4 Go for a walk.   h _ _ _ a walk
5 Put on your clothes.   g _ _ d _ _ _ _ _ _ _
6 Go to the shops.   g _ s _ _ _ _ _ _ _

E What different things can you see? Test! Speaking Part 1

F Let's find A–Z.

91

Unit 44 Which day was it?

A 🔊 CD1:28 Listen and draw the four pictures. What did Alex do last week?

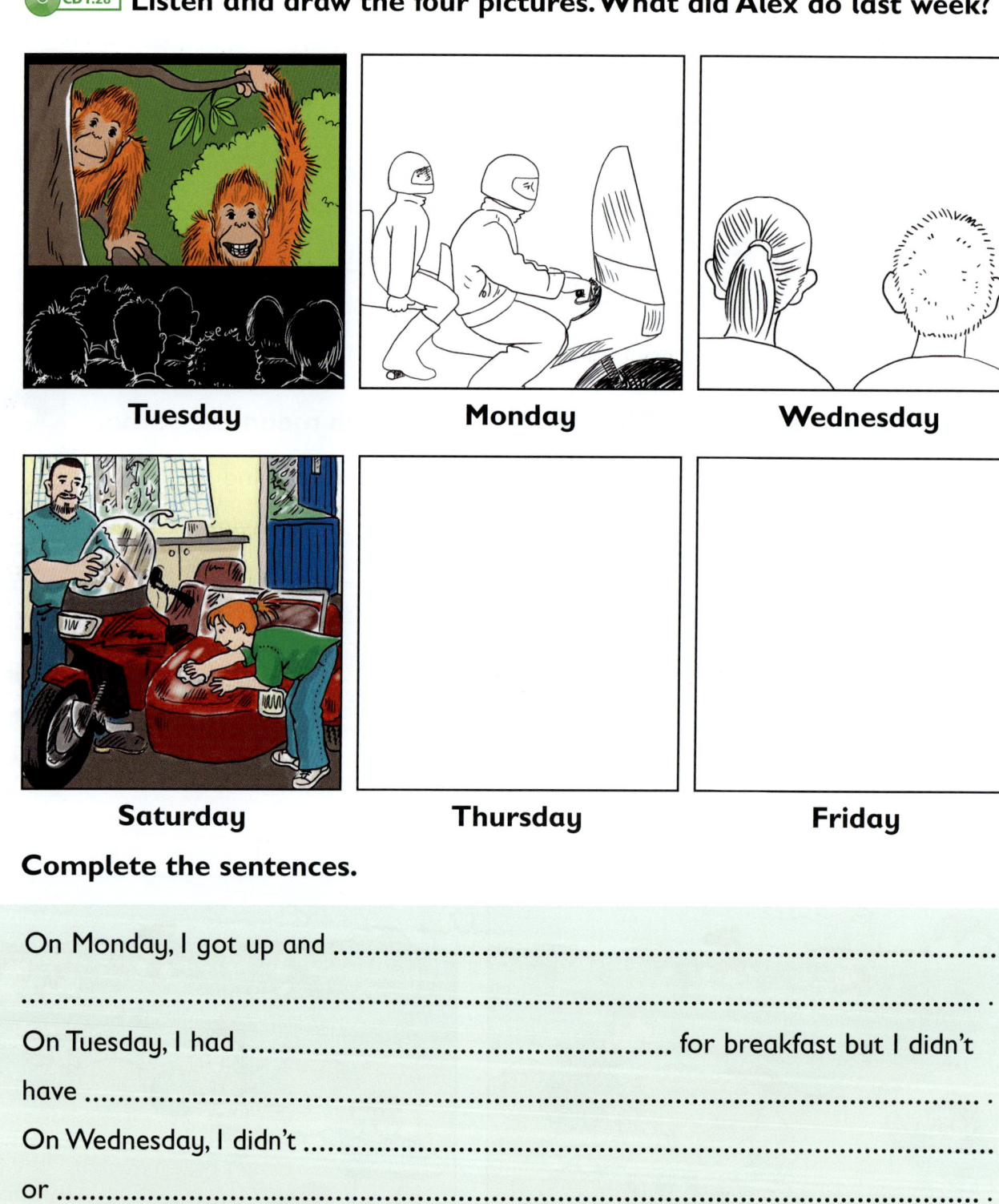

Tuesday

Monday

Wednesday

Saturday

Thursday

Friday

B Complete the sentences.

On Monday, I got up and ....
....

On Tuesday, I had .... for breakfast but I didn't
have ....

On Wednesday, I didn't ....
or ....

Last Thursday I went to .... because ....
....

Friday was exciting because ....
....

C Choose a word from the box. Write the correct word next to numbers 1–5.

Example

nurse   bus   ate   hospital

clothes   saw   night

Hello! My name's Mary. I'm a (1) ...*nurse*... and I work at a (2) .... in the city. Sometimes, I have to work at (3) .... For example, yesterday I woke up in the evening. My family (4) .... fish and chips for dinner, but I had breakfast! I got dressed and went to work, but they took off their (5) .... and went to bed!

Then, in the morning, when I came home on the (6) .... , I had dinner and they had breakfast!

D Look at these pictures. What different things can you see?   Test! Speaking Part 1

E Play the game! Day words and sentences.

93

Unit 45 Treasure

A Look and read. Choose the correct words and write them on the lines.

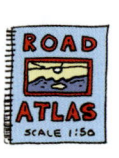

Test! Reading & Writing Part 1

a ticket    coconuts 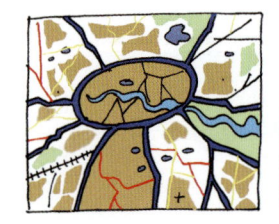   maps    treasure

trees    islands    a pirate    a boat

Example

This person is in stories and sometimes has a parrot!   a pirate

1 You must buy this when you go to the cinema.   ....

2 There are lots of these in forests. They have leaves on them.   ....

3 Look at these when you need to find roads to different towns.   ....

4 These places have water all round them.   ....

5 It's exciting when you find this under water or under the ground.   ....

6 Some people like sitting in this and sailing or fishing.   ....

B Look at the pictures and read the story. Write 1, 2 or 3 words to complete the sentences.

Test! Reading & Writing Part 5

Last Sunday, I went to the cinema with my family. We bought the tickets, then went inside the cinema. We sat down and the movie started. The film was about a famous pirate called Bill. He had a black beard and moustache and was very strong. He had a parrot whose name was Clever. Clever always sat on Bill's shoulder.

94

Examples The boy and his family went to see a film last ....*Sunday*........ .
When the family had their tickets, they ......*went inside*...... the cinema.

1 There was .... in the film whose name was Bill.

2 Bill was very strong and his beard and moustache were ....

3 Clever was Bill's ....

In the film, Bill and his pirates sailed to a small island. When they got to the beach, Bill was hot and tired. 'Bring me some food!' he said to the pirates. 'Find Clever some food too!' Bill's pirates climbed trees and found some bananas, pineapples and coconuts to eat. They all sat down and ate the fruit, then slept on the sand.

4 The pirates went by boat to a ....

5 Bill was .... when he sat down on the sand.

6 Bill told the pirates to .... some food for him and Clever to eat.

7 The pirates all had something to eat, then they .... on the beach.

Bill and the pirates woke up. Clever jumped up and down on some sand and said, 'Treasure! Treasure!' Bill said, 'There's treasure here. Clever is never wrong!' The pirates found the box and laughed very loudly when they looked inside. That night, they sang and danced and played music on the sand.
I loved the film. It was great!

8 Bill knew that there was some .... on the beach because Clever was always right!

9 The pirates .... when they saw the treasure in the box.

10 The boy in the cinema .... the film.

Unit 46 A day on the island

A 🎧 CD1:29 **Listen and draw lines.** Test! Listening Part 1

Sam   Peter   Vicky   Jack

Lucy

Alex

Sally

Now find the differences.

(A) In my picture:

1 the girl is hiding behind a ....

(B) ....

2 a .... bird is sitting on the big boat.

(B) ....

3 the girl is holding her .... because it hurts.

(B) ....

(B) In my picture:

4 the man in the small boat is ....

(A) ....

5 the pirate is holding a round .... mirror.

(A) ....

6 the child who is looking for some glasses is a ....

(A) ....

96

B Look and read. Write *yes* or *no*. Test! Reading & Writing Part 2

Examples

It's a hot and sunny day. ....*yes*..........

One person is swimming in the sea with the shark. ....*no*..........

Questions

1 The woman in the pink dress has got brown hair. ....

2 All the people in the picture have got shorts on. ....

3 There are more than two boats in the sea. ....

4 The boy who's sleeping is wearing a blue T-shirt. ....

5 The parrot is inside the cage that the boy is holding. ....

6 The pirate in the big boat has a black hat on his head. ....

C Listen and make the sentences.

1 ....

2 ....

3 ....

4 ....

D Play the game! Guess my sentence.

Unit 47 Things we do!

A Things I do. Draw lines.

1 answer — j my teacher's questions
2 do   a my best sweater
3 invite   b difficult games
4 put on   c my bike
5 catch   d a train
6 ride   e at funny films
7 laugh   f my friends to a party
8 play   g for the school bus
9 wait   h all my homework
10 drive   i a sports car

B Where do you do the things in A?

in our road   ~~in this classroom~~   round the lake
in my bedroom   in the bank   at the cinema   on my computer

1 I answer my teacher's questions ...... in this classroom ......
2 I ....
3 I ....
4 I ....
5 I ....
6 I ....

C Listen and tick (✔) the box.

1 What's Peter doing now?

A ☐   B ☐   C ☐

2 What's Jane doing now?

A ☐   B ☐   C ☐

D 🎧 CD1:30 Listen and colour and write. Test! Listening Part 5

....

....

E Who is doing what?

1 .... and .... are w.................. !
2 .... is s.................. on a chair.
3 .... is j.................. into the water.
4 .... is w.................. a T-shirt.
5 .... is s.................. in the pool.

F Play the game! Change places.

Unit 48 Round the world

A Read the questions and write a–h next to the correct person.

1 Are you afraid of spiders?
2 Can your father dance?
3 Do your friends like riding motorbikes?
4 Did your mum bring you to school this morning?
5 Have you got a headache again?
6 Would you like to come to the Jungle Cinema?
7 Was your grandpa a farmer?
8 Could you see the ball?

a Yes, I would.
b No, he can't.
c Yes, I am.
d Yes, he was.
e No, I haven't.
f No, she didn't.
g No, they don't.
h Yes, we could.

B Read the text and choose the best answer.

Test! Reading & Writing Part 3

Example
Tom: Hello Jane. What are you reading?
Jane: A Upstairs in my bedroom.
(B) A book about a famous person.
C No, I'm not doing that.

Questions
1 Tom: What did the person in the book do?
Jane: A She sailed round the world.
B What a funny dream!
C I didn't do my homework.

2 Tom: Wow! That's exciting!
Jane: A All right, you can do that.
B No, my boat is old now.
C Yes, she was very clever.

3 Tom: Do you like the book?
Jane: A Yes, I have.
B Yes, I must.
C Yes, I do.

4 Tom: Is it a very long book?
Jane: A No. There aren't many pages.
B I'm sorry. This isn't mine.
C Yes, she had long hair.

5 Tom: Can I read it after you?
Jane: A Well done!
B Yes, OK.
C So do I!

100

C Read the story. Choose a word from the box. Write the correct word next to numbers 1–6.

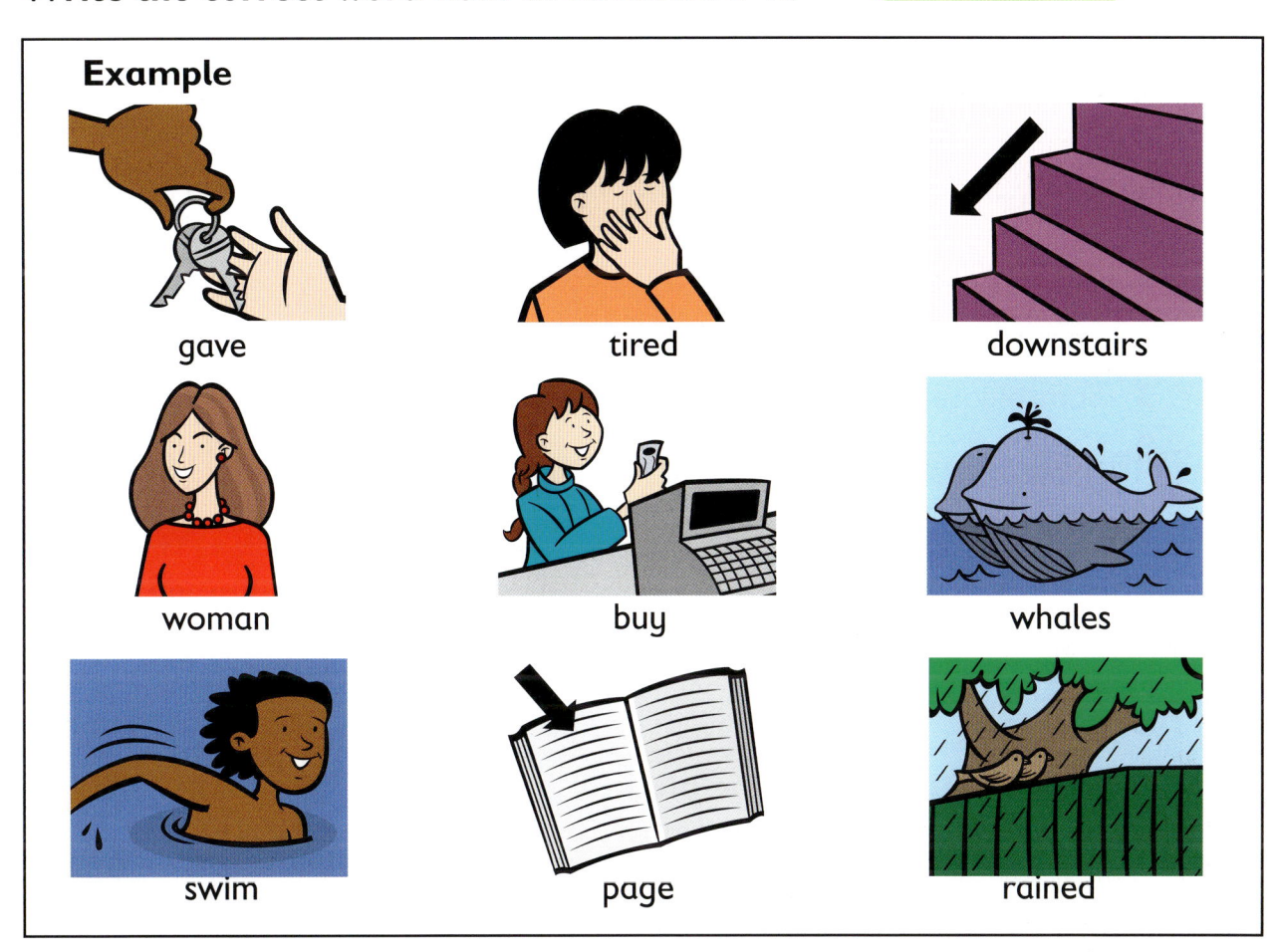

Test! Reading & Writing Part 4

Example

gave · tired · downstairs

woman · buy · whales

swim · page · rained

Jane loves reading. Last Tuesday, her father ......*gave*...... her a new book to read. It was about a (1).................. who sailed round the world in a very small boat. Her name was Mary Banks and she was only 22. It was a very exciting story. Mary saw (2).................. and sharks in the sea. She was often (3).................. but she was never afraid.

When Mary came home, lots of people wanted to read about her. Jane read a story about her on the back (4).................. of one of her comics! Mary was often on television too. Jane loved the book. 'Can we (5).................. a boat, Dad?' she asked. 'I want to sail a boat round the world too!' Jane's father looked at her and smiled. 'I think that's a great idea, Jane. But first you must learn to (6).................. !'

Now choose the best name for the story. Tick one box.

Jane's new boat ☐

Dad gives Jane a present ☐

Mary learns to swim ☐

D Let's see! How well do you know your friend?

Unit 49 — Words you need

A Make sentences with these words.

1. Miss Glass: do / How / you / say / this? .... How do you say this?
2. Sam: don't / I / know. ....
   Miss Glass: Helicopter.
3. Sam: please? / again / you / Can / say / that ....
   .... I don't understand.
   Miss Glass: It's a helicopter.
4. Sam: do / How / spell / you / helicopter? ....
   Miss Glass: H–E–L–I–C–O–P–T–E–R.
   Sam: Thank you.

B Make sentences about the picture.

C   Where are these things? Draw lines to the correct answers.

The coat is — in the cupboard.
The fan is — on the table.
The rainbow is — on the handbag.
The helicopter is — above the sea.
The mouse is — behind the woman's head.
The bottle is — below the clock.
The map is — next to the window.

D   Read the text and choose the best answer.

Example
- **Jane Try:** Hello Paula.
- **Paula:**
  - (A) Good morning!
  - B Thank you!
  - C Well done!

1 Jane Try: How old are you, Paula?
- **Paula:**
  - A Fine, thanks.
  - B I'm ten.
  - C Paula Jones.

2 Jane Try: Who do you play with at school?
- **Paula:**
  - A In the playground.
  - B After lessons.
  - C My friends.

3 Jane Try: What games do you play?
- **Paula:**
  - A My computer is at home.
  - B My dad, sometimes.
  - C We skip and hop.

4 Jane Try: What's your favourite lesson?
- **Paula:**
  - A We're in music class.
  - B Music's the best.
  - C Mr Green.

5 Jane Try: When do you do your homework?
- **Paula:**
  - A After school.
  - B In the library.
  - C With my sister.

E   Listen and choose answers.

F   Answer these questions with the answers you did not choose in D or E.

1 When do you talk to your friends?   ☐
2 Where's your computer?   ☐
3 What's your name?   ☐
4 Who do you go home with?   ☐
5 What are you learning now?   ☐

G   CD1:31 Listen and answer.

103

Unit 50 — Opposites and places

A Write the words you hear. Then complete the sentences.

1 You are not ......**well**......... when you have these. headaches, ...**colds, coughs**......

2 You wear these when the weather is .... coats, ...

3 These people are in your .... your aunt, ...

4 These help you go .... or down to another floor. elevators, ...

5 You can .... things here. a shop, ...

B Read the sentences. Write the words for the pictures on the lines after the sentences.

1 We find these in the bathroom. a bath, ...

2 You need a ball to play these. football, ...

3 You can ride these. a horse, ...

C Play the game! Stepping stones.

Play Stepping stones.

- **the end**
- z: you see animals here
- y: not today
- x: 5 things you can see in the country
- w: not better
- v: smaller than a town
- u: not downstairs
- t: not bottom
- s: 4 places in a town
- r: not weak
- q: not loud
- p: children play here
- o: 3 places with water
- n: not closed
- m: not good
- l: you climb this
- k: not first
- j: a room in a house
- i: another place with trees
- h: not outside
- g: not cold
- f: not terrible
- e: a place with trees
- d: not boring
- c: not clean
- b: not straight
- a: not ugly
- **the start** / not before

105

Unit 4 — The girl in the red dress

Learner A

Let's talk about you and the clothes you wear.

1. What clothes do you like best?
2. What do you wear when it's wet?
3. What **don't** you wear when it's cold?
4. What do you wear at home?
5. Where do you put your clothes when you take them off at night?

Unit 9 — My family

Learner A

Now let's talk about you and your family.

1. How many people are there in your family?
2. Who is the youngest in your family?
3. What do you do with your family at weekends?
4. Tell me about your best friend.

Unit 26 The bats are everywhere!

Unit 11 Things we eat and drink

Learner A

Let's talk about you and food.

1 Who buys the food in your house? ....

2 Do you shop for food at a supermarket, in a shop, or at a market?

   ....

3 What do you have for breakfast? ....

4 What vegetables do you like? ....

5 What's the name of your favourite restaurant? ....

107

Unit 4 The girl in the red dress

Learner B

Let's talk about you and the clothes you wear.

1 What clothes don't you like?
2 What colour are your favourite clothes?
3 What clothes are you wearing now?
4 What clothes **don't** you wear when it's hot?
5 What's the **last thing** you put on before you go out of your house?

Unit 9 My family

Learner B

Now let's talk about you and your family.

1 How many cousins have you got?
2 Who is the oldest in your family?
3 Where do you go with your family on holiday?
4 Tell me about a person in your family.

Unit 33
On your feet and on your head

Unit 39
Lost in the forest

Learner A

Ben's week

	Monday	Tuesday	Wednesday	Thursday	Friday
Morning					
Afternoon					
Evening					

109

Unit 39 Lost in the forest

Learner B

Anna's week

	Monday	Tuesday	Wednesday	Thursday	Friday
Morning		📖			
Afternoon	🏑		🎵		🛍️
Evening				📺	

Unit 11 Things we eat and drink

Learner B

Let's talk about you and food.

1 Who cooks the meals in your house? ....

2 Where do you have lunch? ....

3 Do you help in the kitchen at home? ....

4 What fruit don't you like? ....

5 What food is your country famous for? ....

Unit wordlist

1

animals

bat ....
bear ....
bird ....
cat ....
cow ....
crocodile ....
dog ....
dolphin ....
fly ....
frog ....
goat ....
kangaroo ....
lion ....
lizard ....
mouse/mice ....
panda ....
parrot ....
rabbit ....
shark ....
snake ....
whale ....

body and face

head ....
leg ....
mouth ....
nose ....
part ....
tail ....
tooth/teeth ....
tail ....

the natural world

grass ....
river ....
sea ....
water ....

other nouns

cage ....

adjectives

afraid ....
beautiful ....
big ....
hungry ....
small ....
ugly ....

verbs

can ....
carry ....
catch ....
crack ....
eat ....
fly ....
help ....
jump ....
live ....
open ....
plant ....
run ....
sing ....
sit ....
sound like ....
swim ....
walk ....

111

adverbs

very ....

well ....

2

animals

chicken ....

duck ....

elephant ....

fish ....

giraffe ....

hippo ....

horse ....

kitten ....

monkey ....

pet ....

puppy ....

sheep ....

spider ....

tiger ....

the natural world

farm ....

jungle ....

lake ....

verbs

climb ....

give ....

like ....

ride ....

adjectives

different ....

3

body and face

beard ....

hair ....

people

boy ....

film star ....

girl ....

man ....

people ....

other nouns

glasses ....

kind ....

mirror ....

picture ....

colours

black ....

blonde ....

brown ....

fair ....

grey/gray ....

red ....

white ....

adjectives

curly ....

long ....

short ....

straight ....

verbs

colour ....

draw lines ....

look different ....

make a film ....

paint ....

4

body and face

bottom half ....
eye ....
foot/feet ....
neck ....
top half ....

clothes

coat ....
dress ....
hat ....
jacket ....
jeans ....
scarf ....
shirt ....
shoe ....
skirt ....
sock ....
sweater ....
trousers ....
T-shirt ....

possessions

bag ....
book ....
camera ....
computer ....
fan ....

other nouns

monster ....
picture ....

verbs

carry ....
put on ....
take off ....
wear ....

5

body and face

face ....
hand ....

people

baby ....
boy ....
child ....
friend ....
girl ....
man ....

other nouns

drawing ....
English ....
party ....
playground ....
robot ....
sentence ....

colours

blue ....
green ....
yellow ....

adjectives

clean ....
difficult ....
dirty ....
easy ....
exciting ....
fat ....
favourite ....
funny ....
happy ....
loud ....
naughty ....

new ....
nice ....
quick ....
quiet ....
right ....
sad ....
slow ....
strong ....
tall ....
thin ....
weak ....
wrong ....
young ....

verbs
invite ....
phone ....
talk ....

expressions
Good idea! ....
Here you are! ....
So do I! ....

6

places
cinema ....
city ....
farm ....
hospital ....
road ....
school ....
shop ....
street ....
supermarket ....
village ....

people
woman ....

travel
bus ....
car ....
helicopter ....
lorry ....
motorbike ....
plane ....
truck ....

other nouns
flower ....

7

weather
cloud ....
rain ....
rainbow ....
snow ....
sun ....
weather ....
wind ....

sports
badminton ....

other nouns
painting class ....

adjectives
cloudy ....
cold ....
hot ....
sunny ....
wet ....
windy ....

verbs

choose ....

fly a kite ....

go sailing ....

have an idea ....

paint a picture ....

play badminton ....

rain ....

ride a bike ....

snow ....

expressions

Wow! ....

What a great picture! ....

Well done! ....

What's the weather like? ....

8

the natural world

a country ....

place ....

world ....

time

week ....

verbs

get cold ....

sleep ....

move ....

wake up ....

adjectives

bad ....

best ....

better ....

worse ....

worst ....

9

body and face

back ....

family

aunt ....

brother ....

child/children ....

cousin ....

dad ....

daughter ....

father ....

granddaughter ....

grandfather ....

grandma ....

grandmother ....

grandpa ....

grandparent ....

grandson ....

mother ....

mum ....

parent ....

sister ....

son ....

uncle ....

verbs

be called ....

drive ....

go by car ....

go for a ride ....

love ....

10

people

best friend ....

clown ....

115

grown up ....

possessions

box ....

computer game ....

guitar ....

phone ....

school bag ....

shoe box ....

tennis bag ....

watch ....

other nouns

shop window ....

verbs

learn to play a sport ....

stand ....

wait at a bus stop ....

prepositions

in front of ....

question words

Who? ....

Whose? ....

Why? ....

11

drinks

coffee ....

juice ....

lemonade ....

milk ....

tea ....

water ....

food

bread ....

cake ....

cheese ....

chips ....

egg ....

fish ....

fries ....

ice cream ....

pasta ....

rice ....

salad ....

sandwich ....

soup ....

fruit

apple ....

banana ....

coconut ....

grapes ....

lemon ....

lime ....

mango ....

orange ....

pear ....

pineapple ....

tomato ....

watermelon ....

meals

breakfast ....

dinner ....

lunch ....

meat

burger ....

chicken ....

sausage ....

vegetables

bean ....

carrot ....

onion ....

pea ....

potato ....

places

café ....

restaurant ....

verbs

call ....

cook ....

drink ....

eat ....

shop ....

12

food and drink

bottle ....

bowl ....

cup ....

glass ....

other nouns

birthday party ....

CD player ....

phone number ....

present ....

shelf ....

skates ....

verbs

have to ....

have got to ....

must ....

need ....

adjectives

closed ....

open ....

round ....

square ....

tired ....

prepositions

behind ....

between ....

near ....

next to ....

out of ....

under ....

expressions

Right! ....

13

home

balcony ....

basement ....

chimney ....

door ....

flat ....

floor ....

garden ....

house ....

leaf/leaves ....

lift ....

mat ....

roof ....

stairs ....

tree ....

wall ....

window ....

verbs

bring ....

clean ....

have a wash ....

put ....
watch ....
adverbs
downstairs ....
inside ....
outside ....
upstairs ....
prepositions
above ....
below ....
at the bottom of ....
on ....
expressions
Come on! ....

14
home
address ....
apartment ....
bath ....
bed ....
chair ....
clock ....
cupboard ....
sofa ....
table ....
rooms
bathroom ....
bedroom ....
dining room ....
hall ....
kitchen ....
living room ....
time
weekend ....

other nouns
circle ....
family name ....
star ....
triangle ....
verbs
spell ....
expressions
Bye for now! ....
See you! ....

15
school
answer ....
board ....
bookcase ....
class ....
classroom ....
cross ....
desk ....
eraser ....
homework ....
lesson ....
letter ....
map ....
mistake ....
page ....
pen ....
pencil ....
playground ....
rubber ....
ruler ....
sentence ....
text ....
tick ....

word ....

travel

train ....

other nouns

end ....

verbs

ask ....

come back ....

know ....

make a film ....

show ....

smile ....

understand ....

enjoy ....

point ....

adjectives

correct ....

right ....

wrong ....

16

sports

ball ....

baseball ....

football ....

hockey ....

sailing ....

swimming ....

swimming pool ....

soccer ....

table tennis ....

days

Friday ....

Monday ....

Saturday ....

Sunday ....

Thursday ....

Tuesday ....

Wednesday ....

verbs

go sailing ....

go swimming ....

hit ....

jump ....

kick ....

laugh ....

pick up ....

shout ....

watch a DVD ....

watch a game of football ....

....

adjectives

boring ....

OK ....

expressions

Help! ....

17

hobbies

comics/comic books ....

cooking ....

dancing ....

radio ....

skating ....

clothes

sun hat ....

places

beach ....

sand ....

other nouns

ice ....

story ....

towel ....

verbs

bounce ....

draw pictures ....

jump out of planes ....

play the piano ....

sing ....

wave ....

write a song ....

adjectives

clever ....

18

body and face

arm ....

ear ....

shoulder ....

stomach ....

colours

orange ....

pink ....

purple ....

other nouns

basketball player ....

basketball cup ....

plant ....

shop window ....

verbs

cry

look at your watch

throw

19

health

dentist ....

doctor ....

headache ....

nurse ....

stomach-ache ....

temperature ....

toothache ....

other nouns

movie ....

verbs

have fun ....

adjectives

careful ....

terrible ....

well ....

20

health

cold ....

cough ....

earache ....

other nouns

rock ....

verbs

hurt ....

adjectives

all right ....

fine ....

expressions

Good evening! ....

Oh dear! ....

What's the matter? ....

other words

nothing ....

21

places

bank ....

market ....

shop ....

store ....

the natural world

forest ....

island ....

verbs

buy ....

go on your bike ....

adjectives

thirsty ....

adverbs

down ....

up ....

expressions

Good idea! ....

22

places

bus station ....

café ....

forest ....

library ....

park ....

zoo ....

food and drink

chicken salad ....

soup ....

possessions

handbag ....

other nouns

postcard ....

verbs

catch a bus ....

complete ....

go for a swim ....

go for a walk ....

have a drink ....

talk to your friends ....

expressions

See you! ....

23

the natural world

countryside ....

jungle ....

moon ....

mountain ....

star ....

waterfall ....

verbs

take a photo ....

prepositions of place

at the top of ....

24

other nouns

shopping ....

verbs

cross ....

shop ....

adjectives

awake ....

expressions

Excuse me! ....

Goodbye! ....

I have to go now! ....

Yes, thank you. ....

25

home

armchair ....

possessions

camera ....

kite ....

toothbrush ....

other nouns

laugh ....

verbs

have an idea ....

read a story ....

ride a horse ....

determiners

all ....

lots of ....

expressions

Sorry? ....

26

school

alphabet ....

letter ....

verbs

come home ....

email ....

have dinner parties ....

play loud music ....

play the guitar ....

determiners

both ....

most ....

27

time

afternoon ....

evening ....

every day ....

morning ....

night ....

sports

sports centre ....

tennis class ....

tennis teacher ....

other nouns

age ....

wash ....

work

farmer ....

verbs

clean your teeth ....

get up ....

go shopping ....

have a holiday ....

have a shower ....

have dinner ....

wash the dog ....

wash your face ....

work ....

adjectives

double ....

adverbs

always ....

never ....

often ....
sometimes ....
expressions
Pardon? ....

28
other nouns
email ....
video ....
verbs
catch fish ....
climb mountains ....
film ....
get dressed ....
have a party ....
listen to music ....
make a video ....
sail ....
skate ....
video ....
question words
How often? ....

29
possessions
doll ....
verbs
go for a picnic ....
learn English ....
look for ....
wave goodbye ....
adverbs
badly ....
carefully ....
loudly ....
quickly ....

quietly ....
slowly ....

30
places
post office ....
food and drink
brown bread ....
verbs
help on the farm ....
adjectives
angry ....
left ....
right ....
question words
How old? ....
What kind of? ....

31
food and drink
supper ....

verbs
come home for lunch ....
....
jump into the water ....
....
jump off a rock ....
text ....
visit ....
adjectives
boring ....
exciting ....
naughty ....
surprised ....

expressions

How are you? ....

So do I! ....

32

home

blanket ....

verbs

bounce a ball ....

make a sandwich ....

play football ....

skip ....

wash your hands ....

question words

How many? ....

How much? ....

33

the natural world

sand ....

shell ....

sports

skate ....

other nouns

thing ....

verbs

have a dream ....

hold ....

hop ....

kick a ball ....

listen to a song ....

look at a map ....

34

other nouns

kilo ....

shopping ....

verbs

drop ....

need ....

think ....

adjectives

empty ....

35

time

last night ....

last week ....

yesterday ....

family

baby sister ....

other nouns

paint ....

smile ....

verbs

go by plane ....

go skating ....

take someone in the car

....

expressions

All right! ....

Good night! ....

Tell me more! ....

Well! ....

What about..? ....

36

places
circus ....

people
clown ....

other nouns
kilometre ....

verbs
climb the stairs ....
colour pictures ....
cook lunch ....
dance to music ....
phone a friend ....
sail down the river ....
start ....
stop ....
talk about football ....
work ....

adjectives
busy ....
little ....
missing ....

37

home
hall cupboard ....

people
driver ....

other nouns
work ....

verbs
get up ....
put on clothes ....
say goodbye ....
take a bus ....
take off clothes ....
wake up ....

expressions
Be careful! ....

38

work
bus driver ....

clothes
uniform ....

verbs
buy a present ....
clean a bike ....
do homework ....
draw a map ....
drive a bus ....
get home ....
go to a party ....
live in the countryside ....
open a letter ....
ride to work ....
tick the box ....

expressions
Good morning! ....
Here you are! ....
Hurray! ....

39

work
policeman ....

verbs
hide from someone ....
look for ....
lose ....
try to find ....

125

want ....
question words
When? ....
Where? ....

40
possessions
CD ....
lamp ....
toy car ....
other nouns
birthday ....
birthday present ....
cinema ticket ....
verbs
close your eyes ....
have some cake ....
have a stomach-ache ....
make a cake ....
make the dinner ....
expressions
Let's go! ....
Me too! ....
Thanks! ....
What a nice day! ....

41
food and drink
a piece of cake ....
chocolate ....
home
elevator ....
verbs
drive a lorry ....
drive a truck ....

wash the floor ....
expressions
Fine! ....
Great! ....
How about some juice? ....
....
OK. ....
Would you like an ice cream? ....
....

42
sports
sports lesson ....
possessions
photo ....
verbs
bring home ....
give ....
go on holiday ....
take with you on holiday ....
....

43
other words
example ....
something yellow ....
verbs
have a swim ....
have a walk ....
mean the same ....
stop laughing ....
adverbs
first ....
then ....

44

verbs

come home on the bus ....

go out ....

go to bed ....

listen to the radio ....

see a film ....

watch TV ....

work at a hospital ....

work at night ....

45

animals

parrot ....

people

pirate ....

possessions

map ....

ticket ....

treasure ....

verbs

buy a ticket ....

climb a tree ....

go by boat ....

46

clothes

shorts ....

other nouns

difference ....

verbs

fish ....

47

travel

sports car ....

verbs

answer your teacher's questions ....
....

laugh at funny films ....

wait for the bus ....

write email ....

48

verbs

be on television ....

bring to school ....

dream ....

learn to swim ....

meet a film star ....

sail round the world ....

49

school

music class ....

verbs

take a test ....

expressions

Fine, thanks. ....

Good afternoon. ....

How do you spell that? ....
....

Pardon? ....

50

verbs

go to a different floor ....

prepositions

after ....

before ....

Irregular verb list

Verb	Past simple	Translation
be	was/were	....
bring	brought	....
buy	bought	....
can	could	....
catch	caught	....
choose	chose	....
come	came	....
do	did	....
draw	drew	....
dream	dreamt/dreamed	....
drink	drank	....
drive	drove	....
eat	ate	....
find	found	....
fly	flew	....
get	got	....
get dressed	got dressed	....
get undressed	got undressed	....
get up	got up	....
give	gave	....
go	went	....
have	had	....
have to	had to	....
hide	hid	....
hit	hit	....
hold	held	....
hurt	hurt	....
know	knew	....
learn	learnt/learned	....

Verb	Past simple	Translation
lose	lost	....
make	made	....
mean	meant	....
put	put	....
put on	put on	....
read	read	....
ride	rode	....
run	ran	....
say	said	....
see	saw	....
sing	sang	....
sit (down)	sat	....
sleep	slept	....
spell	spelt/spelled	....
stand (up)	stood	....
swim	swam	....
take	took	....
take off	took off	....
tell	told	....
think	thought	....
throw	threw	....
understand	understood	....
wake up	woke up	....
wear	wore	....
write	wrote	....